The Louisville Story

BY
OMER CARMICHAEL
AND
WELDON JAMES

SIMON AND SCHUSTER
1957

LIBRARY OF CONGRESS CATALOG CARD NUMBER: 57–10971
MANUFACTURED IN THE UNITED STATES OF AMERICA
BY KINGSPORT PRESS, INC., KINGSPORT, TENN.

TO THE

Children of Louisville

AUTHORS' NOTE

IN OUR *collaboration on this book we came to share a belief that "The Louisville Story" could best be told as though the Superintendent of Schools were telling it, and so in the text every "I" lacking quotation marks may be attributed to him.*

We share also a strong belief that no two communities are identical, that no plan of social change workable in one can be imported by others without amendment or improvement. The complex problems of each differ in nature and in degree from those of any other. Certainly the people of no two cities are ever quite alike. But we believe that the likenesses nevertheless are as profound if not as sharp as the differences, and that there is no community of Americans that cannot with profit observe the doings of another—just as Louisville has benefited from close study of the ways in which other cities have solved or sought to solve the problems posed by any program of public-school desegregation.

It is a pleasure to acknowledge our great debt to the Fund for the Advancement of Education, without whose support this project would not have been possible. And our debt to many Louisvillians, especially among the staff of the public schools and the management and personnel of the Louisville newspapers, is too great to be detailed.

It is our joint hope that this small volume may serve not as a blueprint for any other community but as a cheerful stimulant to the thinking of men of good will everywhere.

OMER CARMICHAEL
WELDON JAMES

CONTENTS

Contents

The
Louisville
Story

► I ◄

△

The Quiet Heard Round the
World

LACK OF CONFLICT does not often make the headlines.
But in Louisville on September 10, 1956, against
the din of conflict elsewhere, there was such a mighty
quiet that people heard it not only in the White House
but in every corner of the world. It shone forth from
the television screens of the nation. It made headlines
not only in the New World but in the Old World as
well, in Europe, in Asia, in Africa.

Aside from the press, the President of the United
States was the first to inquire into the why and how of

3

it. He hoped the why and the how of it might make good sense to others. And others came to Louisville, as the quiet continued in the ensuing months, to ask the same questions the President had asked in the White House—others from all over the United States, from Europe, from Asia, from Africa.

For what had happened in Louisville on September 10—or what had not happened—was of unique interest to all the races of mankind. Against the clamor of racial conflict elsewhere, it was a triumph—small, perhaps, and inconclusive, perhaps, but still a triumph—of man's ability to solve some of his most vexing problems with reason and good will.

In other American communities that day and that week and that month the news was not so good. Some of them, like Louisville, were trying to comply with the ruling of the United States Supreme Court that in our constitutional democracy the guarantee of equality of citizenship meant that racial segregation in the public schools must end.

In the great majority of these, it is worth remembering, there was no trouble. More than 600 school districts changed their racial rules in 1954–56 without disorder, scores of them in Kentucky in 1955–56, where communities like Frankfort and Lexington, to name but two, were models of smooth transition.

But in some of them last fall, unlike Louisville, the news was not of quiet but of conflict: of angry mobs, of naked racial hatred, of state troopers and National Guardsmen restoring uneasy order at the point of the bayonet, the threat of the machine gun, the rumble of the tank.

All of the front-paged news was from the South, from Texas, from Tennessee, from other communities in Kentucky—states among the seventeen directly affected by the Supreme Court's ruling. But on page 18 or thereabouts of the Chicago newspapers you might discover that there, too, the threat of violence to the first five Negro pupils admitted to one erstwhile all-white high school was ominous enough to require a police escort for the Negro pupils, week after week, no matter how long a history of supposedly desegregated schools the state of Illinois had enjoyed. Trouble between the races, as always, knew no geographical boundaries but only the hearts of men.

Louisville was luckier.

But no one, in the suspenseful days of early September, would have bet too much on that luck.

We had made the most conscientious preparation for the day of change that it was in our power to make —the day when race alone would bar no child from any Louisville school, the day when some of the customs and traditions of centuries would end, the day when the new era bespoken by the Supreme Court would begin.

But other communities had made conscientious preparation, too—some of them. Yet September already had brought trouble and violence to some, sometimes where only a handful of Negroes were involved.

In Louisville it was not a matter of handfuls. Pupil registration completed the week before had shown 12,010 Negroes among the total of 45,841—roughly one in four, or nearly 27 per cent, the highest in any great city initiating a desegregation program in 1956.

And the foes of the program had promised bitter opposition—the legal opposition of picket lines and demonstrations that so quickly had led to the illegality of violence elsewhere.

There was good reason to believe, too, to put it mildly, that most of the people of Louisville were no more enthusiastic about the impending change than are people anywhere when confronted with profound alterations in their way of life. And from what had happened elsewhere, not merely in September but in the darker years before, came the grim knowledge that when peoples of different races are involved it takes but a minor spark to set off a major explosion—if enough people so will it.

The people of Louisville, white and black, willed otherwise. There was no explosion.

This is the story of those people and their city, of what they were doing to better racial relations in the years before the Supreme Court spoke, of what their school officials and their civic leaders and churchmen and the press and the people themselves did in twenty-seven months to prepare for the day of transition, of what has happened since. Not, as I explained to the President, a story of one man, or even of a few, but of many; not of a school system only, but of a whole

6

community. And it is the story of what now, in 1957, pupils and parents and teachers and preachers and politicians and just plain people have to say about the past, and the present, and what they think they can see of the future.

It is not all good. Nothing in it approaches perfection. And the story has not ended.

But it is far better than many had dared to hope.

► II ◄

△

Something about a City:
Gateway to the South

<hr>

BACK IN 1937 a writer for *Harper's* took a good look at Louisville, still numbed by the great flood of that year, and reached a grim verdict. To George R. Leighton it was a city of let-well-enough-alone, a mere museum piece where no "genuine intellectual life" could flourish. Gateway to the South, as it had grandly claimed to be virtually since its founding in 1778, the old city beside the Falls of the Ohio was living on its sentimental recollections of a great past: *rigor mortis* had set in.

Ten years later Harold H. Martin of *The Saturday Evening Post* tarried in the "rich, proud, friendly old brick-and-limestone town" long enough to report more optimistically. Things were humming. One week a year, he conceded, the city put on the time-honored mask of Ol' Cunnel Louisville—courtliness, hospitality, goat-whiskers, bourbon-breath and julep talk, Southern drawl and all—and played host, at a somewhat embarrassing profit, to the hundred thousand visitors who help to make the Kentucky Derby what it is. But for the rest of the year, though the fast horses and the fine bourbon and the beautiful women were not ignored, the mask was dropped. Louisville had "performed prodigious labors" in the 1941–45 war effort, expanded her old industries, attracted many new ones. Something called the Louisville Area Development Association was busily working on the present and planning for the future. Its directors included "representatives of all the town's diverse interests, opinions and prejudices—Democrats, Republicans, the old conservative rich, the new progressive rich, labor, big industry, small industry and the Negro." Civic and cultural improvement were the goals of postwar Louisville. Already much had been accomplished, and Mr. Martin approvingly quoted one citizen's conclusion that "Louisville seems to be moving, almost without knowing it, into a considerably better future."

In 1955 *Harper's* sent a man down for a fresh look. People living in Louisville found it a little difficult (as they had in 1937) to recognize themselves and their

9

city in the resultant portrait. But William Manchester's materialistic oils were heavily mixed with cultural and civic flattery, and few resident viewers could resist the temptation to see in the finished portrait a considerable resemblance to reality. Picking up where Mr. Leighton had left off, Mr. Manchester found that the city had "staged a spectacular comeback, rising, in less than two decades, from stagnation to prosperity —and it has done it without tax cuts, cheap labor, or other sycophantic gestures toward Yankee industry." And the decisive factor had not been those eternal assets of central geographic location, the nearness of the Kentucky coal fields, and the transportation-booming Ohio River. "The decisive factor," said Mr. Manchester, "is both new and unique. Here is the only American city which has ever used culture as an industrial agent. Louisville has succeeded where other Southern cities have failed, because it has deliberately made itself a pleasant, stimulating place to live."

Aside from the detailed millions represented by great new industries, new schools, new buildings for the University of Louisville, new four-lane expressways (one "significantly" named after Henry Watterson, editor of the *Courier-Journal* for fifty years), the great floodwall, improved acoustics for a municipal auditorium now happily host to Broadway plays, and so on, Mr. Manchester found far more to extol.

"Despite its sudden growth," he declared, "the new Louisville prefers to think of itself as the home of musicians and bibliophiles—a place where the local

10

philharmonic orchestra outdraws the university basketball team and a public-library card entitles the holder to take out any reasonable number of books, five long-playing records, a feature-length film, a framed painting—and, if it is raining, an umbrella."

With a low bow to Robert Whitney and the world-famed Louisville Orchestra, to Clarence R. Graham and the nationally famous library system he runs, to the Louisville Fund's importance as a kind of Community Chest for the arts, and to Dr. K. P. Vinsel, the one-time political science professor and football coach, who as executive director helped forge the union of several organizations into a Chamber of Commerce representing both industry and labor, Mr. Manchester came up with "the theory behind all this" and a partial list of the men responsible.

The theory: "That industries which are really desirable want decent homes and cultural facilities for their employees—and the city's rising skyline suggests that the theory works." The men responsible for the fact that the city's development is not blind but is being planned: "Men who are convinced that its greatest resource is a reputation for intellectual vigor. . . . In Louisville—thanks to a strong two-party system, a local tradition of public service, and an enlightened newspaper—they run things. They include a liberal publisher; a mayor determined to end racial segregation; two distinguished former mayors; and the executive director of the Chamber of Commerce."

Any vigorous-minded Louisvillian could lengthen

11

that list—or shorten it. But that can pass. Implicit in most such "outside" views of Louisville is its identification as a Southern city, no matter how near the Midwest or true Yankeeland may be, no matter how rapid the recent pace of industrialization, with the consequent importation of mobile Americans from all over. Great numbers of the white newcomers, for that matter, and smaller numbers of Negroes, are Southerners —not merely from the old "Confederate counties" of Kentucky itself, but from Louisiana, Mississippi, Georgia, the Carolinas, and, as of old when Kentucky was but a frontier county of the Old Dominion, from Virginia.

And there is good reason, despite its basic character as a border city in a border state, for Louisville's invariable impression of Southernness. A century ago it was one of the great slave-trading centers of the Old South—and kept its slaves for nearly a year after the Emancipation Proclamation. Though the Union held it during the War Between the States (to the city's profit as an important base of supply for the Western campaigns), its people divided like the people of all Kentucky; in the gentle hills of Cave Hill Cemetery the tourist today can see the mute reminder of how brother fought against brother. Colonel Thomas H. Hunt, C.S.A., returned after Appomattox to sell his undamaged mansion on Walnut Street and move to the more purely Confederate climate of New Orleans —but his action was hasty. Louisville, like Kentucky,

12

it has been said, seceded after Appomattox: the freeing of the slaves, their overnight enfranchisement, and the vengefulness applied to the Reconstruction of the conquered South led most Kentuckians straight into the Democratic Party and a sharper social identification with the South. Though Louisville itself long has had a strong two-party system, with a healthy balance of independent-minded voters, only twice in a century have Kentucky's citizens given a clear majority to Republican candidates in a national election (1928 and 1956). Louisville's voters matched the national pattern in liking Ike in 1956, and they have been represented in Congress by a Republican for a full decade—but they have entrusted their local affairs to a series of distinguished Democrats without interruption since 1933. The truth is that innumerable Louisvillians, to the despair of all party managers, often vote Democratic locally, Republican nationally. The rest of the South, of course, had a cousinly brush with this tendency in 1952 and 1956, not to mention 1928.

Politics aside, Louisville has faced South since 1865. Its customs and its outlook have been almost professionally Southern. It is the Confederate ancestors who dominate all social resurrection. Families of every political persuasion, old and new, have richly honored the traditional injunction to serve the public interest. The monument of the stalwart Confederate rifleman on Third Street is not matched by that of a Unionist anywhere in the city. And in 1956 hardly anyone in

Louisville could have been surprised by a transplanted Carolinian's feeling that he had found a second home where "the best of the Old South" lived on.

Yet no citizen of Louisville could deny that its status as a border city long ago brought it a dividend of incalculable worth: a climate of tolerance, of live-and-let-live, of deep respect for the law. It had to achieve that climate or perish, as it learned in the anarchy of the Know-Nothing riots against Catholics a century ago, in the awkward years when defeated Rebels yoked with triumphant Unionists to build a greater city, in the long decades of adjustment to fresh waves of immigration from Germany, from Ireland, from the Deep South and North and the Middle West.

It is a climate that takes a lot of tending. But Louisville's true wealth is the great number of hands available for the task.

Today's Louisville is a bustling, sprawling city of 412,000, heart of a metropolitan area of 669,200—larger by 46 per cent than in 1940, the Chamber of Commerce likes to remember, and likely to hit the million mark by 1980. Its growing pains and problems are familiar enough to its sisters throughout the land to need no mention here, save for a deep local share of the national complaint: overcrowded classrooms, insufficient first-rate school plants, and more crowding to come.

Of the 412,000 people in the city, 65,920 are Negroes —16 per cent, but accounting for nearly 27 per cent of the public-school enrollment of nearly 46,000. The school proportion is due, in great part, to the fact that Louisville's Catholics (30 per cent of the city's population) support a parochial school system enrolling more than 23,000—and few of the city's Negroes are Catholics.

Louisville's Negro community is not unlike the Negro community in many another city, North and South. Its population has increased in recent years (10,499 in one decade), while the state's Negro population was decreasing (by 12,110). As in most Southern cities, Negroes live in every one of Louisville's twelve wards. But as in many Northern cities, most of them are concentrated in a few predominantly Negro areas. Some are wealthy, or well-to-do, and well educated, and there is a large class of able lawyers, doctors, educators, ministers, and businessmen. But the bulk of the Negro population, as University of Louisville sociologist Robert I. Kutak reported last November, is concentrated in areas of low social and economic status. Two-thirds are renters, compared with fewer than half of the white population. Their median income is about $1,000 less than that of whites. Discriminatory practices in hiring, Dr. Kutak found, keep large numbers of Negroes in the less skilled and less well-paid occupations. The homicide death rate in a recent year was 56.3 per thousand among Negroes, compared with 3.2 among whites. The death rate from natural causes is 50 per cent higher for Negroes than whites, and Negro deaths due to tuberculosis alone ("a disease associated with poverty") outrun the

white rate three to one. It is still true, as an Urban
League survey put it in 1948, that Louisville's Negroes
"live in poorer houses than whites, are arrested more
frequently, and die earlier." And in the public schools
it is a fact, as Dr. Kutak reported in 1956, that "Negro
students are more retarded than are white students"—
though this is due "not to the fact that the students are
Negro, but that most Negroes live in areas of low
socio-economic status; white students who live in these
areas are also retarded."

Louisville is also a city of churches and synagogues
—more than 600 in the city and its suburbs. Some
313,000 people are on their membership rolls. More
Negroes than whites, proportionately, are church
members—nearly two thirds of the total Negro population.

Louisville is a city of colleges and seminaries, too.
The University of Louisville, founded in 1837, enrolls
some 6,000 in its many schools and adult education
centers. There are three small Catholic colleges, Ursu-
line and Nazareth for women, Bellarmine for men.
The Southern Baptist Theological Seminary and the
Louisville Presbyterian Seminary draw ministers-to-be
and missionaries-to-be from all over the world. And
Georgetown College, Kentucky Baptists' senior liberal arts institution in Georgetown, Kentucky, will
soon open a Louisville division.

All of these facts and these impressions, and the impact they have on men's minds, are relevant to one

question: How would such a city go about the business of erasing the color bar in its public school system?

The first answers come from what had been happening in Louisville before the Supreme Court's historic ruling of May 17, 1954.

► **I I I** ◄

△

The Changing Times:
Before the Court Spoke

___

No FUNCTION of government—not even the collection of taxes—touches so many people so closely
as does the operation of the public schools. Touch the
schools and you touch the mass of the people, for in
a democracy like ours no other institution stems so
directly from the people themselves.

To schoolmen and school boards that fact is inspiration in itself. But it can also be cause for tribulation;
for everything that happens to the people of any community can have a direct effect on their thinking and

their feeling about their schools, and so, in time, on the schools themselves. It should be enlightening, therefore, to take a quick look at what the people of Louisville were doing and saying about race relations in the years before the Supreme Court made public school desegregation mandatory.

Until a fleeting yesterday, Louisville's racial customs and laws, with two important exceptions, were virtually identical with those throughout the South. The exceptions: the city in modern times has never required segregation in public transportation, and the right of Negro citizens to vote has been exercised freely for many decades. Otherwise, by custom or law or both, strict segregation long was the order of the day in public and private life alike.

The record of gradual change in recent years, particularly in the decade ending in 1954, included the opening to Negroes of the Louisville Free Public Library and its branches, the University of Louisville and the Catholic Colleges, the public golf links, the student nurses' home of General Hospital (operated by the City-County Board of Health), the end of enforced segregation at the Greyhound Bus Terminal, the assignment of Negro firemen to previously all-white fire stations, the admission of the first Negro members to the Jefferson County Medical Society and the local bar, the opening of the Louisville Park Theatrical Association's programs to "anyone who wants to buy a ticket." These changes in 1948–54 had their roots, of course, in preceding years of a long period of

19

amicable relations between the races, and they were to be followed by other changes in the following two years; some of them by court decree or following the threat of legal action, others without pressure.

All of them suggest, from a record only part of which needs to be detailed here, some conclusions of obvious significance to any community on the threshold of desegragating its public schools: (1) In a decade of great changes in racial relations largely decreed by the courts, Louisville in some cases "read the handwriting on the wall" and acted without legal compulsion, in one or two others proceeded without enthusiasm but also without disaster to comply with the law; (2) Both before, during, and after that decade there were strong influences in the community supporting the changes as just and right, and responsible leaders of both races, as the sociologists would put it, never "lost communication"; (3) Relations between the races, uncomplicated by boycotts, ultimatums, or peremptory demands on the part of Negro leaders or by hostile or inflammatory statements from "the Confederate Democrats" in City Hall, remained basically good.

Which is not to say there was not argument, controversy, and litigation—as well as peaceful persuasion and, sometimes, reluctant adjustment to the inevitable. The story of Louisville's famous park system, with most of its more than 2,000 acres reserved for whites, is a case in point.

It was only ten brief years ago—brief to the gradualist or the detached student of history, an admitted eternity to the impatient, or, as the old saw has it, to the man behind bars—that Louisville's racial arrangements in the parks headed for the courts. In the hot summer of 1947 four Negro ministers asked Mayor E. Leland Taylor to permit Negroes to use all the city parks.

"I agree with your statements that legally and morally you are entitled to the same rights and privileges as Louisville's white citizens," Mayor Taylor told the delegation. "But at the same time I will not take the responsibility for setting a precedent which, I am convinced, would touch off a race riot. Compared to other cities Louisville has had exceptionally good race relations. The colored people of this community have their own Chickasaw Park. If I were to throw open the other parks to them, it would give the hoodlums of both races the opportunity they seek to cause trouble —trouble which would engender bitterness and hate that would take years to overcome."

Subsequently a Negro dentist, with legal assistance from the National Association for the Advancement of Colored People, filed suit in Jefferson Circuit Court. His immediate target was the Parks Director. The Parks Director cited a 1924 resolution of the old Parks Board, passed after some disorders in the parks, that it was "not desirable or safe for whites and Negroes to use the same parks and swimming pools," and held that its successor since 1942, the Department of Parks and Recreation, had continued the policy. He proposed that the Board of Aldermen restate policy on "this hot potato." But it was one of those rare times when Louisville had a Democratic Mayor and a Republican majority on the Board of Alderman, and the aldermen decided, with due dignity, that it was up to the mayor.

In the ensuing litigation Col. Carl Heustis, then and now Chief of Police, testified that desegregating the parks could bring added trouble to the undermanned police department, requiring it to go on 12-hour or even 24-hour duty. Before the year was out Circuit Court ruled that the Negro dentist was seeking "a social and not a political right." The Kentucky Court of Appeals later upheld this ruling, and the Negro attorneys began a long battle in the federal courts. In 1948 a new Mayor, Charles Farnsley, subsequently active in ending segregation in several fields, gave an interracial delegation of college students small comfort on the parks issue: he would feel the public pulse on the matter, he said, but would not promise to be bound by the results. "Segregation," he said, "is a serious problem. It has been argued for several thousands of years and I don't know all of the answers." But he thought his record showed, he said, that he had been "fair and sympathetic in dealing with the problems of Negroes."

The delegation included white students from the University of Louisville, Negro students from the Louisville Municipal College. But a spokesman for the University of Louisville Student Council said that

22

the University was not to be "drawn into the matter," because the Council, composed of the elected representatives of the student body, had voted 8 to 6 against making a protest over park segregation.

Nineteen hundred and forty-eight was the year, of course, when Harry S. Truman was opposed for the Presidency not only by the G.O.P. candidate, Thomas E. Dewey, but also by the Progressive Party's Henry A. Wallace. The local political fireworks, in terms of racial relations, were brief but illuminating. The Progressive-sponsored Civil Rights Committee of Louisville and Jefferson County announced plans for an interracial picnic in Shawnee Park "to prove that mixed groups can meet in peaceful and friendly fashion."

But the campaign-time picnic was called off when committee members claimed to have discovered that they would be "walking into an organized massacre by a band of hoodlums, organized by certain low elements seeking political advantage." A committee spokesman identified the "low elements" as Republicans. G.O.P. campaigners rejected the charge as "ridiculous," and the Democrats tacitly agreed. It was a "Communist goon squad," warned Safety Director McCandless, that was planning to incite a race riot at the picnic. And Mayor Farnsley said this in a letter to the committee:

"You are doubtless aware of the fact that your proposal has precipitated a heated controversy and this office has received numerous letters displaying active, hostile sentiments against the Negro race. It therefore seems to me your proposed picnic might well be the starting point of disorders of a grave nature which would result in a serious setback to those of us who are working for improved race relations."

Reading of the letter at a committee meeting drew some withering remarks, but the committeemen decided to cancel their picnic plans because "violence would not help the cause for which the committee is fighting." Opponents of the cancellation included James Wilson, a Negro photographer. "I've got a kid," he said. "If I don't fight for his rights, who will?" And he complained bitterly that "Negroes are only half-men," barred not only from the white parks but from theaters, restaurants, and other public places.

The long park-opening litigation fared differently in the federal courts. In 1950 Federal District Judge Roy M. Shelbourne excluded action against the Louisville Park Theatrical Association, a private agency sponsoring summer opera in the Iroquois Park Amphitheatre, but said he would have to rule on the action against the city. It was, he said, "not a question of segregation, but of deprivation." And in 1951 he ruled that Louisville must either let Negroes play on city-park golf courses and fish in Cherokee Park Lake or give them similar facilities substantially as good as those used by white people.

So it was that in 1952 the color bar disappeared on the golf courses and at the lake. But the bar stayed up in other parts of the park system, and there were more suits. In 1953 the city helped to celebrate its 175th anniversary by sponsoring Barbara Anderson's moving version of *The Tall Kentuckian* at the Amphitheatre in Iroquois Park, and since this tribute to the Great Emancipator was not available in all-Negro Chickasaw Park or the six smaller parks open to all, Mayor Farnsley decided that Negroes should be allowed to attend the three-week performances in Iroquois. Negro attorneys contended that if the city could amend the segregation ordinance for three weeks there was "no reason for the rule at all any more," and lost another case in Circuit Court. But the following year the directors of the theatrical association voted to sell tickets to "anyone."

In 1954, after seven years of recurrent and still unfinished litigation, Louisville's major parks and all its swimming pools were still segregated.

Before and during this period of legal conflict some notable changes occurred with a minimum of controversy.

Organization of the interracial Louisville Urban League in 1920 had ushered in a period during which the community became increasingly aware of the social and economic problems of the Negro minority. The League, enlisting the support of leaders of both races, gradually achieved concrete improvement in opening new economic opportunities to Negroes. This goal was furthered, beginning in the 1940s, by considerable though not unanimous labor union support. In the field of community welfare the League cam-

paigned successfully for the assignment of funds, services and personnel on the basis of need rather than
racial numbers.

And it kept constantly before the community, as
commentary on its revealing surveys and its programs
for change, the contention of its interracial leadership
that "the problems usually designated as racial are
fundamentally the problems of low economic status
and are the responsibility of the community as a
whole." In 1948, as the winds of change began to blow
more strongly throughout the United States, the
League warned whites and Negroes alike of specific
dangers they faced—the whites of "a patronizing attitude born of the belief they are doing something for
Negroes over and above their responsibility as members of the community," the Negroes of "becoming so
obsessed with their own plight as to lose perspective
and balance and becoming utterly blind to their obligations to the community as a whole."

New educational opportunities for Negro citizens
opened up in 1928, with establishment of the Negro
Catholic High School on a tuition-free basis by the
Archdiocese of Louisville, and the opening in 1931 of
the Louisville Municipal College, a segregated branch
of the University of Louisville. (Since 1904 Kentucky's
Day Law specifically had prohibited all institutions,
public or private, from mixing races in the classroom
at any level.) Enrollment in the Negro Catholic High
School (now, in 1957, about 75) never exceeded 125,
in Municipal College seldom more than 300. But the

latter represented, in the spirit of the times, an attempt by the university trustees to live up to the "separate but equal" educational doctrine endorsed by the Supreme Court in 1896.

One small event in 1935 had considerable effect on later interracial developments: Louisville elected the first Negro to sit in the Kentucky Legislature, Charles W. Anderson, Jr.,—and in Frankfort this Republican, re-elected regularly until he resigned in 1946 for another "first" as Assistant Commonwealth's Attorney in Louisville, developed a close association with his next-desk neighbor, Democratic Charles Farnsley. In the postwar years Farnsley was twice to serve as Mayor of Louisville, and to have a profound influence in desegregating its university and its public libraries.

Mayor Wilson Wyatt in 1942–1946, before he became President Truman's Housing Expediter, took two steps that paved the way for greater change. Soon after his election he appointed several Negro leaders to a postwar planning commission for the city, and in 1943 he appointed a Negro to the public library's board of trustees. The trustees in 1948, when Farnsley was mayor, voted to open the main branch of the library to Negroes—and in 1952, after four years in which some predictions of racial tension had been gathering dust, the color bar was lowered in the library's branches throughout the city.

The library chief, Clarence (Skip) Graham, gave major credit for the smoothness of this change, plus the planned development of a rich cultural life available to all citizens, to the creation of "an aura of tolerance" in Louisville.

The Civil Service

In the city's civil service, change was more gradual —and more sweeping. Negro policemen, firemen, and garbage collectors have been on City Hall's payroll for decades. But it was not until 1943 that Safety Director Joseph F. Donaldson, in doubling the size of the Negro force, for the first time named three Negro police sergeants. Both actions, Donaldson said in a public statement, were "continuation of established policy and were prompted by the merit shown by colored officers."

Shortly afterward a Negro honor graduate of the Louisville Municipal College, Mrs. Amelia Ray, became the only Negro member of the city's Crime Prevention Bureau. And on October 9, 1949, Safety Director David McCandless, later to become director of the University of Louisville's Southern Police Institute, announced appointment of the first Negro police lieutenant, Augustus W. Edwards—on the basis of civil service examinations and long service as a sergeant.

It might be worth noting in passing that Louisville's Negro policemen, unlike those in some cities, are empowered to arrest offenders of any race.

In the training of nurses city authorities as long ago

as 1941 got a "go ahead" opinion from the State Attorney General's office that the Day Law would not apply to instruction in the city-operated General Hospital. Negro nurses were already serving on the hospital staff, but had been trained elsewhere. Subsequently a semi-integrated training program developed there, at the Red Cross Hospital for Negroes, at the old Louisville Municipal College and then the integrated University of Louisville. In his 1953 campaign for the mayoralty, Andrew Broaddus pledged complete desegregation in this field, including the admission of Negroes to the nurses' home at General.

Hospital officials at first thought it might be better to "ease into the situation," as one member of the City-County Health Board put it. Encouragement of Negro girls to live elsewhere, they thought, might avoid a possible decline in applications for training. But in December Mayor Broaddus publicly reiterated his demand: "I feel there should be no distinction," he said. "They (Negro students) are just people, and should be treated exactly like the others."

The younger generation, he added, "doesn't think like we with the gray hairs do" about racial questions. At its subsequent meeting the board decided to go along with Mayor Broaddus, but that no official action was required because it had never formally laid down policy in this area. The bars went down.

(That was the year in which two Catholic hospitals, following the example of St. Joseph's Infirmary the year before, opened their nurse-training to Negroes.

One of them, St. Anthony's, reported no Negro applicants. But SS. Mary & Elizabeth Hospital had eight Negroes in a 28-member class, and reported that, living together in the regular student nurse quarters, "the white girls accept the Negroes very beautifully.")

It was in January 1954 that Mayor Broaddus climaxed two decades of changing policies in City Hall's hiring-and-firing policies with a brief announcement. Henceforth all city jobs, he said, would be open to Negroes who could qualify for them. He told civil service officials to stop specifying "Negro" or "white" in ads for applicants for civil service jobs in city departments and agencies. And in non-civil service agencies and departments (employing about half of the city's 4,200 workers), he ordered officials to hire applicants according to their qualifications for the job regardless of race.

Higher Education

Of all the changes in interracial arrangements before 1954, none had greater impact on the community than the desegregation of the University of Louisville in 1950 and the fact that, two years later, President Philip Davidson could describe the university's experience with the process as "magnificent."

In 1949 the federal courts had ruled that the University of Kentucky must open its graduate and professional schools to Negroes. Many other institutions at the time, of course, were adjusting their admission practices to principles enunciated by a Supreme Court on which Kentucky's Fred M. Vinson, as every Louisvillian knew, sat as Chief Justice. But the University of Louisville acted without the pressure of litigation the moment that amendment of the state's segregation law allowed.

Mayor Farnsley's Legislative Committee drafted an amendment measure, and the Louisville delegation in Frankfort worked diligently for it in both House and Senate. The bill in its first draft provided that Negroes might attend public and private institutions of higher learning in Louisville, but was revised to apply to all Kentucky. It stipulated two conditions: Negroes might attend higher educational institutions (1) if the institutions' governing bodies approved and (2) if comparable courses were not available at Kentucky State College for Negroes.

Opposition in Frankfort was bitter but not strong. Said one opponent in the House: "We're too far South to mix the races in the schools." Rep. Morris Weintraub, Newport Democrat, countered that "we must do away with bigotry and prejudice not only in this country, but all over the world." And House Majority Floor Leader James P. Hanratty of Hopkinsville concluded: "Even if you don't like it (nonsegregation in the schools), it's the thing that's coming. It's developing right along." The House approved, 50 to 16, the Senate 23 to 3, and Governor Earle C. Clements signed the bill into law.

It was a measure that quickly enabled the University of Louisville, the city's three Catholic colleges, the Southern Baptist Theological Seminary, and the Louisville Presbyterian Seminary to open their doors to Negro students—not to mention a majority of the state's other similar institutions, public and private, in the ensuing years. But the unique position of the University of Louisville in the community, and the obvious influence of its experience on community thinking, make its story worth detailed examination.

The University's initial step was taken after a poll of the general public indicated that 49.4 per cent opposed admission of Negroes, 39.4 per cent favored it, and 11.2 per cent had no opinion.

The University story can best be told in the words of Vice-President Woodrow M. Strickler, who addressed them to the 10th National Conference on Higher Education in Chicago in the spring of 1955, when the Louisville public schools were preparing their desegregation program—and when Mr. Strickler's words were pondered by many a reader of the Louisville newspapers.

The University's trustees, Mr. Strickler recalled, had voted to admit Negroes to graduate study the moment that amendment of the state's segregation statutes permitted. That was in 1950. The following year all racial barriers were lowered, and the University estimated that by closing the old Negro Municipal College branch, its annual savings were $50,000 or more. It was the first university in the South to enroll Negro undergraduates and to hire a Negro faculty member —Dr. Charles H. Parrish, Jr., professor of sociology.

The University was "pretty worried" about all this in 1950, Mr. Strickler said, but had found its "trepidation" totally unwarranted:

"The University has endured many emergencies during the past five years, but none of these emergencies has had a basis of racial conflict."

And he added:

"Negro fraternities and sororities have been organized. Negroes have attained positions of campus leadership. They live in dormitories, attend university classes, and play on varsity athletic teams.

"The only difficulty the university has faced has not been the fault of the Negroes. The institution rents a swimming pool for swimming classes and uses parks for botany classes. The organization owning the swimming pool prohibits attendance of Negroes; city parks are operated on a segregated basis. Consequently Negro students must be prohibited from these classes or classes abandoned.

"The problem has been solved satisfactorily by simply asking Negro students not to enroll in classes using rented facilities, or by asking them to be certain to work out substitute measures with their teachers, as in the case of the botany classes.

"Evidence has been presented in some institutions

that Negro students have been handicapped by an inferior educational background. . . . In the experience of the University of Louisville this problem has had little importance, because a vast majority of the Negro students come from a large Negro high school which is equipped and staffed in every way to prepare qualified students adequately for college-level work. This condition has operated to prove that there is no racial basis for inferior performances.

"For the average white student, the appearance of Negroes as classmates and participants in student activities has had little, if any, significance. They have been sympathetic or indifferent. Negro students have been accepted in direct proportion to their capacity for contributing to student life.

"When the process of desegregation is as abrupt as it has been at the University of Louisville, where almost overnight a Negro college was closed, its property sold and its students absorbed in other schools of the University, it can be expected that Negro faculty members will, for an interim period at least, very likely lose their jobs as teachers. . . .

"If Negro schools are abolished, it seems inevitable that some qualified faculty members will be forced from the teaching profession, because it is likely that colleges and universities will continue to lag in adding Negroes to their faculties in the same proportion as they add white people. On the other hand, it seems plausible that, as the demand for qualified teachers continues to grow, the displaced Negro teacher will find a proportionate increase in the number of job opportunities available to him. . . .

"Negro citizens will continue to contribute in increasing measure to the planning and operation of programs of higher education. It is necessary that this be so, because only in this way can many of the complicated problems of desegregation be solved intelligently and without incident."

There is a pre-1954 footnote worth adding about the state's Day Law. Amended several times, as it had been, it still prohibited racial mixing in elementary and secondary schools, public or private. In 1951 the Mayor's Legislative Committee endorsed legislation to let non-tax-supported schools in Kentucky admit Negroes. It did so on motion by the Rt. Rev. Felix N. Pitt, secretary of the Catholic School Board. Monsignor Pitt said that passage of the bill would probably end segregation in some and possibly all Catholic high schools in Louisville and Jefferson County, and certainly in the two under direct jurisdiction of Archbishop John A. Floersch, head of the Catholic School Board.

But the 1952 Legislature failed to approve the measure. And the 1954 Legislature, though the House in March of that historic year voted 52 to 32 in favor of a similar bill, never finished the job. It was a great disappointment to three Louisville Democrats who had sponsored the measure—Mrs. Thelma Stovall, now Kentucky's Secretary of State; the Rev. Felix S.

Anderson, a native of North Carolina who at the time was the only Negro member of the General Assembly, and Senator Leon J. Shaikun. But some senators didn't see much point in bringing the bill to a vote: everybody knew that the Supreme Court of the United States would soon rule one way or the other on school desegregation, and they felt they might as well wait for such clarification.

There might be a pre-1954 footnote, too, about other individuals and organizations in Louisville actively engaged in bettering racial relations or urging adjustment in racial custom—or both.

For many years, of course, the YMCA, the YWCA, and the Urban League had sponsored programs and activities—many interracial in character—designed to promote good race relations. Under Barry Bingham as president and Mark Ethridge as publisher, the *Courier-Journal* and the *Louisville Times* since 1936 had given vigorous editorial support to the same goal. They had campaigned with equal vigor for a full measure of justice to all citizens regardless of color. Local radio and television handling of racial issues in most cases reflected some of the same ideas. And then, in the five or six years immediately preceding 1954, three new organizations played a well-publicized part in encouraging better communications between the races.

They were the spiritual descendants of the old Committee for Interracial Co-operation in Louisville —formed soon after World War I and eventually affiliated with the Southern Regional Council. Committee

leaders in those distant days included Patrick Calla-
han, an eminent Catholic layman and philanthropist;
Mrs. Emmet Horine, of the Louisville Council of
Church Women; Dr. Julian Price Love, of the Presbyterian Seminary; Dr. E. A. McDowell, of the Baptist
Seminary; Rabbi Joseph Rauch; and, among Negro
leaders, Bishop George Clement and other members
of his family, the Reverend James Bond, the Reverend
John Little, the Reverend William H. Sheppard, I.
Willis Cole, and others. Some of these, with a newer
generation of Louisvillians, helped establish the Kentucky Council on Human Relations in 1954. But before that their pattern of interfaith and interracial co-
operation had extended to larger groups in Youth
Speaks, Inc., the Eastern Council for Moral and Spiritual Education, and the National Conference of
Christians and Jews, a regional office of which was
established in Louisville soon after World War II.

The N.C.C.J. sponsored a series of human relations
institutes each year, all interracial. One involved
teachers only, about 800 of them. There were forty
discussion groups of about twenty members each, and
each group had both Negro and white teachers. In
each institute, Negro and white leadership was used
both in the discussion groups and in the report sessions.

"Youth Speaks," which by 1957 had won three Freedoms Foundation awards, was organized by a representative cross-section of church, school and civic
leaders to offer a forum to all Louisville youth groups

for voicing their deepest concerns and convictions. Its annual feature has been an all-day conference in one of the schools, with 600 to 700 articulate representatives from all high schools in the city and county—public, private, parochial, Negro and white.

The Eastern Council, organized by parents, school patrons, teachers and church workers living in the eastern section of Louisville and Jefferson County, soon found improved racial relations among its moral and spiritual concerns. After its first interracial panel discussion all its meetings were desegregated, and its publicized programs on good human relations had a definite impact on community thinking.

For these and others making major contributions to improved human and racial relations—and therefore to the preparation for school desegregation—the feeling of some was expressed by former Mayor Wilson Wyatt, chairman of Kentucky Brotherhood Week in 1952. Mr. Wyatt cited the election of Negroes to public office and the abandonment of segregation in various educational institutions and civic activities as some of the "many advances in intergroup relations during the past decade." Mr. Wyatt added:

"The doctrine of equality found in the Declaration of Independence was not only the spirit of '76, it is the spirit of brotherhood today.

"Brotherhood and equality, the force which toppled thrones and tyrants in the nineteenth century, remains today the dynamic force which motivates the Western free world.

"We can only achieve peace when we achieve, among ourselves, the principles of brotherhood.

"The principles of brotherhood are principles to be lived daily. Each of us can make, by our own actions, a contribution toward the elimination of bigotry and hatred."

Louisville's Schools

For anyone who had been superintendent of the city's public schools since 1945, it was a professional duty to be aware of all these developments—local, regional and national. Their logical trend toward the Court climax of 1954 could surprise no schoolman or parent who had read the newspapers and the magazines and sometimes the texts of court decisions. The great currents of change in America's political, economic, moral and religious attitudes toward racial problems had long been visible. They contributed to at least a few changes in the Louisville schools during this period. But before we discuss these changes it might be worth while to put our situation in its Kentucky context.

There were no schools for Negroes at all in Kentucky before 1866. In that year the general assembly levied a 5¢ tax on the property of Negroes for the joint benefit of Negro schools and adult Negro paupers. The yield from this amounted to only 6¢ per child, and the following year the legislature boosted it with a head tax of $2 on every male Negro above eighteen, and gave first claim on the money to Negro schools—the remainder still going to pauper relief. Next year the law was amended to give pauper relief first claim—and there was no provision compelling local trustees to establish schools for Negroes.

In 1870 the legislature repealed the old law and applied to Negro property owners the same taxes applied to whites. But again there was no requirement for the establishment of colored schools. It was not until 1874 that Frankfort created a system of common schools for Negroes—financed by specific levies on Negro-owned property, a $1 head tax on all Negro males twenty-one or older, and the income from Negro-paid fines, license fees, penalties, deeds, etc. The act provided for three Negro trustees in each school district, with final control of the Negro system vested in the State Board of Education.

That particular system lasted eight years, during which the white tax structure yielded from $1.25 to $1.90 per child a year. The Negro tax structure netted 30¢ to 58¢ per child a year.

In 1883, by popular referendum, this divided system was replaced by one based on the broad principle of equal taxation and equal support—a principle written into the 1891 state constitution and still in effect.

This new system remained completely segregated, however, although only by unquestioned custom. But in 1904 the Day Law, enacted at a time when Berea College was the only institution in Kentucky with mixed classes, made racial segregation compulsory in private schools and colleges and the public school system alike.

The only notable change in Louisville's segregated system came in 1941, when a racial differential of 15 per cent in teachers' pay was eliminated. In some parts of Kentucky, incidentally, the differential in the old days was sometimes as high as 51 per cent.

When I came to Louisville as Superintendent of Schools in 1945, Negro and white teachers worked in separate groups, whether for general meetings or for committee work. But gradually we made the transition from separate to mixed committees and meetings —always on a permissive basis.

An illustration of this permissiveness might be helpful. In 1950, for example, nineteen textbook-adoption committees were needed. We decided that each committee should have seven teachers, five white and two Negro. But no one was assigned to serve. All were invited. In the letter of invitation each teacher was told to feel free to decline the invitation, to which was attached a list of the proposed members of all nineteen committees. There was no reference to race, but since each member of each committee was identified by the school in which employed, all knew which teachers were white and which Negro.

Of 95 white teachers invited to serve, four asked to be excused, two for health reasons and two, as they frankly put it, because they would prefer not to work on a committee with two Negroes on it. Both indicated regret that they felt this way and said they would serve if we thought they should—but they were excused, and made to feel perfectly "secure" about it.

At staff level in 1948 we employed a Negro teacher as assistant supervisor of music. While her actual supervision was in the Negro schools, she had her office in the administration building along with other supervisory and administrative personnel and, of course, participated in administrative and supervisory conferences. Subsequently, other Negroes were employed by the central office in clerical and other office duties.

The teachers of Louisville, Negro and white, thus had gained valuable experience in working together before 1954. And there were a few Negro employees in our central office. Otherwise the school system was as completely segregated as it had always been.

And as late as 1949 a public opinion poll made by the University of Louisville Psychological Services Center indicated that that was the way most Louisvillians wanted it. The poll covered attitudes toward high school desegregation only. Asked whether they thought that Negroes should be allowed to attend all of the city's high schools, 18.1 per cent said "yes," 7.2 per cent had "no opinion"—and 74.7 per cent gave a resounding "no."

And on June 27, 1954, a few brief weeks after the Court's ruling, there was violent racial trouble in a

Louisville suburb. Dynamite blasted the home of a Negro newly moved into the all-white subdivision of Rone Court—a mystery still not solved in 1957, and the after-effects of which echoed in the headlines for many months.

Two things happened a few weeks before the May 17, 1954 Supreme Court ruling that had, I like to think, a definite effect on the course of what was to follow.

One was a public statement of mine anticipating the Court's action, guessing that it might allow from two to five years for completion of compliance, and stressing our readiness to accept it as the law of the land.

Many people have asked me—particularly in recent months—if I was not "sticking out my neck" to issue such a statement without the formal approval of my board. The explanation is simple. I conceive it to be the duty of the Superintendent of Schools to accept the obligations of leadership. I was sure that the board was in complete agreement with such sentiments. There was the possibility that if there were members who were hesitant to crystallize their own viewpoint, this statement might be a timely factor in inducing and strengthening the board's unanimity of purpose. Subsequent events were to prove, as I fully expected, that the Board of Education would be a tower of strength to the entire administrative staff amidst the uncertainties of the next two years.

The other event stemmed from the good intentions of some church people in New York who wanted to assist Louisville in preparing for desegregation. Representatives of their church came to my office—after considerable quiet preparation had been made with some local assistance—to invite me to attend a community meeting with other citizens interested in smoothing the period of transition.

In a long conference I thanked the committee for the invitation. And my thanks were sincere. But I told them I would not attend the meeting and would discourage any friends of mine from attending, because it would harm more than it could possibly help. As kindly as I could, but equally firmly, I explained why. I felt it was up to the people of Louisville to work out the problem themselves—and that they would resent outside leadership, no matter how able or well-meant.

After the Court Spoke:
1954–1956

The Day the News Came

THE MOST IMPORTANT THING that happened in
Louisville on May 17, 1954, was the prompt and
clear-cut acceptance of the Supreme Court desegregation decision as the law of the land, accompanied by
the announced determination of the Governor of Kentucky, the Board of Education and myself, as Superintendent of Schools, to comply with the law.

No community is an island unto itself, much as some
would like to be. Louisville is no exception. It was of

the utmost significance to our local situation that Governor Lawrence W. Wetherby and other state officials, not to mention Kentucky's representatives in Congress, accepted the Court's decision as binding.

In Frankfort, Governor Wetherby said succinctly: "Kentucky will do whatever is necessary to comply with the law." Attorney General J. D. Buckman, Jr., said the ruling nullified the famous Day Law and a constitutional requirement for separate schools—an effect his office later explained would not be final until the Supreme Court's "how and when" ruling later.

In Washington, Kentucky's Congressional delegation, split between majority Democrats and minority Republicans, said nothing to discomfort Frankfort. Democratic Senator Earle C. Clements observed that "Kentucky and Kentuckians have always respected our highest Court and I anticipate orderly steps will be taken to do so in the instant case." Republican Senator John Sherman Cooper found the Court's decision "a logical result of the Constitution" and, although he foresaw some difficulties, expressed the belief that "with good sense and judgment they can be worked out." There were no hurrahs among House members, and one called the decision "most unfortunate," but he agreed with the others in essence: "The Court has decided and that is final."

The historic effect of such statements, coupled with their reiteration by others later, was to eliminate school desegregation as a partisan or factional issue in Kentucky politics.

In Louisville it happened that the Board of Education was in a regular meeting when the news from the *Louisville Times* was read to the members by Board President William C. Embry.

Mr. Embry promptly declared: "Our thinking and planning must start right now even if the decision allows us five years to carry out desegregation."

The newspapers that day quoted these earlier remarks of mine:

"There will be problems but they are not insurmountable, as the integration of Negroes at the University of Louisville testifies.

"The group to suffer most will be the Negro children in the early stages of integration.

"The real problem will be with the adults, however, not the children."

I also said that day that "the pressure is off so far as the effective date of desegregation is concerned. The Court has given us time for an orderly, systematic study."

The day happily brought forth a solidarity of opinion at the top of the educational structure of the metropolitan area that was of obvious importance.

County Board of Education Chairman Richard I. McIntosh said: "I can see that there will be difficulties arising but I don't think we will have any trouble surmounting them in Jefferson County."

County Superintendent Richard Van Hoose said: "We have anticipated the Court's decision to some extent. Now that we have it, we can move forward with more definite plans."

And Monsignor Pitt, secretary of the Catholic

School Board, said ". . . these difficulties can be minimized if all exercise prudence and discretion, understanding, and, above all, charity."

There was another meeting of consequence that day. George Cordery, president of the Louisville branch of the National Association for the Advancement of Colored People, hailed the decision as "a great victory for our people," and presided at a mass meeting of his organization that night. There were some demands for immediate or overnight desegregation voiced, but they never won majority support. Instead, during the next two years, despite occasional individual impatience, Louisville's articulate Negro leadership showed helpful restraint and moderation in allowing the desegregation process to develop uncomplicated by impetuous or intemperate demands for speed.

In its editorial columns next morning, the *Courier-Journal* declared that "people everywhere could well match the Court's moderation and caution." And in the editorial it quoted this historic dissent to the original "separate but equal" ruling of 1896 by Justice Harlan, a Kentuckian and a former owner of slaves:

"Our Constitution is color blind, and neither knows nor tolerates classes among citizens . . . the destinies of the two races are indissolubly linked together, and the interests of both require that the common government of all shall not permit the seeds of hate to be planted under the sanction of the law.

"What can more certainly arouse hate, what more

certainly create and perpetuate a feeling of distrust between these races, than state enactments which in fact proceed on the ground that colored citizens are so inferior and degraded that they can not be allowed to sit in public coaches occupied by white citizens?"

It was the Harlan view, as the *Courier-Journal* put it, "that came to prevail, little by little over the years."

The Louisville Program: Toward a Favorable Climate

Louisville was in an auspicious position to tackle the problem of school desegregation. It had made gradual progress in its adjustment of racial relations in several fields. Powerful voices in the community were prepared to speak up for greater progress.

Nevertheless, the history of public school desegregation in other communities made one thing plain. This was that preparation for so radical a change had little hope of success unless it was a community-wide program.

In the schools, thanks to our belief that the Court's desegregation ruling was inevitable, we had already done some spade work. Our administrative staff had initiated informal exploratory discussions on desegregation the preceding year. We had talked with educators in areas where segregation had existed until fairly recently—notably in Indiana, Pennsylvania and New Jersey. We had "read up" on the subject, and were beginning to develop some tentative ideas.

We knew that we had at least a year, and possibly two, in which to hammer out a program for our community.

It seemed to me that the wisest place to begin would be with the principals and the teachers in our school system—first to define, study and discuss the problems and later to encourage the proposal of possible solutions—and then to encourage the entire community to do the same.

Here perhaps I should explain—considering how many times I have been asked about this on the lecture platform and in educational conferences—why we did not appoint a citizens advisory committee to assist us. The answer in brief: it did not seem necessary. Such committees have been invaluable in some communities, I know. In recent years we have used citizen committees very helpfully in other areas of school work. But in Louisville we had already passed the stumbling block of so many communities—that of deciding to comply with the law. And we felt certain that, working with teachers, pupils and the community, our staff should be able to come up with a program that the Board of Education and the community alike could endorse.

At the beginning of the 1954–55 school year, we began the campaign which I hoped would create a

climate of opinion favorable to the smooth desegregation of our schools. All administrative and other
central office personnel and all principals were asked
to become as fully informed as possible on the question. Principals were asked to arrange faculty meetings and get the fullest possible co-operation of
teachers in studying the question. It was suggested
that, for the first semester, discussion be primarily for
the purpose of discovering and clearly stating problems which, in the judgment of each faculty, should
be considered when the time came to develop a specific program.

The reports of these faculty discussions, a stack of
which looms high in central office files to this day,
were revealing. They uncovered no facet of the problem not already known to communities with experience in school desegregation. But they made all of us
personally acquainted with the problems that we
might expect. One principal summed up a lengthy
report with these words: "We have talked a lot about
this subject. All of it has helped our attitudes."

The problems posed by the teachers, virtually
identical with those later posed and discussed by
request by the various Parent-Teacher Associations,
will be dealt with later. But it is worth reporting here
that, as one might expect, not all the teachers were
enthusiastic about the prospective program. The
great majority reflected a helpful willingness, but the
dissenters, in at least two cases, were as articulate as
any segregationist could like.

Said one, in an unsigned paper after a faculty discussion:

"It seems that the Negroes are dictating to the white people. Why doesn't our Kentucky governor join with the Southern governors and keep our schools segregated?

"To have our white teachers teach the Negro children is to me a bitter dose. What will this lead to? Negro teachers probably teaching white children and even Negro teachers teaching in white schools and vice versa. What white teacher wants to hobnob with a Negro teacher? I don't, to be sure. The idea is simply repulsive.

"It is probably all set up and my idea doesn't count. Therefore this letter is simply wasted even thinking about segregation in public schools."

Another note was equally vehement:

"Are schools in Kentucky ready for this drastic step of race integration? I think not.

"First—Kentucky already rates high in illiteracy. Although we have a few Negroes who are fighting for equality and unity, there are thousands who do not want it. Some have told me so. There are many who will drop out of school altogether because of social inadequacy, thus making our percentage of illiteracy soar still higher. Why should the humble Negro suffer because of the few autocratic ones who lack foresight?

"Second—With a mixed racial class in the schools, our standards of teaching will be pulled so far down that Kentucky will be staggering for at least a decade to get her head above the water.

"I believe in giving the Negro race equal opportunities but in their own schools, taught by their own race.

"I do not feel it wise or even possible at present to take this drastic step of mixing the whites and Negroes in a school classroom in Kentucky. I do not consider it a step forward, but a backward step causing much confusion, turmoil, regret and unhappiness to both races."

Such sentiments were by no means confined to an anonymous handful of teachers, of course. There was reason enough to believe that large numbers of people in the community shared them. Public opinion polls over a period of years and irate letters in the letters columns of the local newspapers were some indication. How widely they might be backed up by dangerous emotionalism we could not know. But we could hear the angry thunder of hardening resistance farther South, and we could read, in that fall of 1954, about racial troubles in Baltimore and Washington and elsewhere. And we believed that the educational process of study and public discussion would work some helpful changes in community attitudes, as it was already doing in teacher attitudes—even if, in some cases, it came out as only willingness to accept, though still to dislike, the inevitable.

So our teachers worked on their own knowledge and attitudes, and they worked with their pupils.

The aim was to get all of them, Negro and white, to go more than halfway to make desegregation work when it came. Some schools added to their libraries many books about Negro children and Negro people for the children to read and enjoy. The strangeness of one group to the other was lessened by the presentation of assembly programs in white schools by pupils from Negro schools and vice versa. Closer working relationships were developed between the two groups by the appointment of joint committees to prepare programs for presentation to Negro and white schools alike. And in some Negro schools, at the suggestion of their principals, there were "good manners contests" and special lessons in cafeteria behavior, health, safety, and good study habits.

"The Negro child," as one principal put it, "will encounter difficulties. It is my idea that he should be prepared to meet them and to help to meet them he should strive to be superior along some lines such as conduct, good manners, proper enunciation, better study habits, etc."

We had little apprehension about the attitude of younger children or of many of the older pupils; we knew that racial prejudice is unknown to the very young. We knew that parents—and grandparents—would be the more difficult problem. But we wanted to do our best to achieve a climate in the classroom that could help affect the temperature outside.

Early in 1955 the Parent-Teacher Associations of the city were asked to arrange meetings in their respective schools for full public discussion of the question. Their instant co-operation was remarkable—and remarkably effective.

Mrs. Herbert Zimmerman, president of the Louisville Council of P.T.A.s, put it this way to council members:

"Our job in P.T.A. is to work for harmony among parents toward desegregation. We should emphasize to them that all races can work co-operatively and effectively. Our aims are the same—better schools, adequate pay for teachers, and the welfare of all our children."

Some P.T.A.s had one meeting, some as many as five. The speakers came from members of the administrative and supervisory staff and some of the principals and teachers, from members of the Board of Education, from the churches, from civic leaders and other interested citizens. The Kentucky Council on Human Relations, under the leadership of Dr. Hugh Brimm, head of the Carver School of Missions and Social Work (affiliated with the Southern Baptist Theological Seminary), provided several. And some P.T.A.s, of course, provided their own speakers and discussion leaders.

As this ferment of useful activity developed, churches and church-related groups, women's clubs, civic clubs and other organizations began to arrange meetings on desegregation. The speakers, as I just observed, came from a variety of sources—and I do not mean for one moment to imply that all of this community activity was solely sparked by the school authorities. Far from it. But we welcomed and encouraged it, and our people spoke at every opportunity. I myself made some sixty platform appearances in this campaign, to groups of a handful or in the hundreds.

In virtually every meeting, the talk was followed by a question-and-answer period. This sometimes lasted as long as two hours. Because parents were deeply interested, the questions were frank and to the point—and certainly the answers from our school people were equally so. Consistently thorough reporting of such meetings by the local newspapers helped us to reach far larger audiences than were in the meeting halls. And the radio and television stations of the city were generous in giving time for programs on desegregation—and for many a panel discussion that they themselves created, like the "Moral Side of the News" panel on WHAS. This particular program is a Louisville favorite in which the news and its implications are discussed by a regular panel that usually includes Dr. Duke K. McCall, President of the Southern Baptist Theological Seminary, Rabbi Joseph Rauch of the Temple Adath Israel, Monsignor Pitt of the Catholic School Board, and the Rev. Robert T. Weston, minister of the First Unitarian Church. Its guest list in this period included Negro ministers, and its agenda always included, when desegregation developments were in the news, "the moral side."

And what was said at all these meetings, and what were the questions asked?

From my own experience I shall try a little later to summarize some answers and to record some representative excerpts of what other Louisvillians were saying during this period. But first, for the possible help of other schoolmen or citizens faced with a comparable situation, let me list a few of the basic tools —aside from our own staff studies, attendance of various staff members at community relations seminars, planning sessions and the like—that proved invaluable to us.

One was Harry Ashmore's gold mine of information, *The Negro and the Schools*. Another was its companion from the University of North Carolina Press, *Schools in Transition*, by Robin M. Williams, Jr., and Margaret W. Ryan. One showed the full scope of the problem (and to my mind the crying need for action to solve it), the other the way in which only yesterday communities from New Jersey to Arizona tackled it with varying methods and varying degrees of success. There is no point to reviewing either book here. There is some point to saying that without a study of both nobody today is fully prepared to discuss the school desegregation problem, much less to attempt to hammer out a workable solution.

And then there was—and is—*Southern School News*, the monthly magazine established immediately after the Supreme Court's 1954 decision to report factually and objectively and in depth on the effects of that decision.

Written and edited by Southern newspapermen, controlled by the Southern Education Reporting Service whose board includes noted Southern editors and educators with personal viewpoints ranging from integrationist or gradual-integrationist to diehard segregationist, this magazine from its first issue has been a treasury of continuous information on what has been happening in all areas affected by the Court's decision. I took one look at its first issue (it was free in those days), and promptly had it sent to every one of my staff assistants, every member of the Louisville Board of Education, and to the local P.T.A. Council president—then subsequently to all supervisors and principals, the president and secretary of every school P.T.A., members of the governing board of the P.T.A. Council, the Mayor and the members of the Board of Aldermen, a few other community leaders, and all ministers and many religious officials in Louisville, Protestant, Catholic, and Jewish.

The Louisville circulation alone of *Southern School News* shortly exceeded 600. And individual copies were passed on to such an extent that they reached hundreds more. When the magazine later changed to a cost basis, I ordered it sent to all members of our administrative staff—and I know that numbers of others ordered their own subscriptions.

It was the full and objective reports of this magazine on desegregation developments everywhere that sparked our community-wide discussion and study of our own desegregation program. They gave us a wealth of information on programs that failed or succeeded in other communities, on the successes and occasional failures of moves to resist or circumvent the Court's order, on what people everywhere were saying and writing about the problem as they saw it.

It gave us in a special field the solid information without which wisely informed action is impossible. And its stories of failures and successes elsewhere reinforced a conviction we had already begun to form: that overnight and unplanned desegregation most often came to grief, that careful planning and informed public discussion of the issues could most often precipitate a climate favorable to change, even when many people were not enthusiastic about change.

Our own program of community discussion had scarcely begun—and with no specific plan of desegregation yet formulated—before I got a well-intentioned letter from a Louisville resident lately come from New Jersey.

In her home town there, she said, much credit for a successful desegregation program had been given to the lack of advance discussion or publicity. Summed up, her theory was that the less said the better—and the less trouble to be encountered later.

She added that her child had been taught by a Negro teacher in New Jersey and that nowhere had she found a more dedicated teacher: "As in the case of white teachers, character and trust command respect before skin color, and so it was there. I cannot accept that human beings in Kentucky are any different from human beings in New Jersey, therefore it follows that what can be accomplished there can be accomplished here. Those who look for problems to settle in the change-over are creating problems."

In my reply I expressed genuine appreciation for her thoughtful advice and said that I was particularly grateful for what she had to say about her experience with a Negro teacher, but I added:

"I cannot agree with the point of view you express that perhaps the best approach to the question is to avoid too much discussion of it and plunge into it. Although it is a question about which people will feel as well as think and reason, and too often feel more than think and reason, I still believe we will be wise to have thorough preparation made by having free discussion in as many groups as practicable before we begin the transition program."

The Shape of the Problem: Questions and Answers

It is not news that a majority of Louisville's Negroes are poorer, less well-fed, less well-housed, and less healthy than a majority of Louisville's whites. It is not news that the Negro percentage of juvenile delinquency is higher than the white. It is not news that the Negro child, on the average, lags considerably behind the white in scholastic achievement.

It is not news that some white people dislike or even hate Negroes—and that some Negroes fully reciprocate. It is not news, either, that what might be a simple altercation between persons of one race can be the occasion for violent mass reaction if one of the antagonists is white and the other Negro.

In our 1954–56 preparations for desegregation, we did not dodge these facts. They were, indeed, the ground from which nearly every question in our question-and-answer sessions developed.

At meeting after meeting I encountered these questions and gave these answers:

QUESTION: Can't we get around this thing some way —why can't we put it to a general vote?

ANSWER: The Supreme Court's decision is the law of the land, and we are therefore bound by it. It will be my purpose to implement that decision with no effort to sidestep, no effort by subterfuge or sharp practices to defeat the purpose of the Court. And don't come pleading to us not to do anything. I tell you frankly we will give you courteous consideration, but the answer is "no." We try always to be courteous. We will not do anything to thwart the law of the land.

QUESTION: Since there is a higher incidence of venereal disease and other illnesses among Negro people, what are you going to do about it?

ANSWER: There is a higher incidence of such diseases among lower white socio-economic groups as well. The basic problem belongs to the community at large and to its health authorities. In the schools we shall maintain our normal health and sanitation standards and our exclusion of any pupils when suffering from infectious or contagious diseases.

QUESTION: Won't mixed classes lead to more mixed marriages?

ANSWER: That's not a school problem—but I don't see why it should. It hasn't in Northern cities with a long history of integrated schools. Most Negroes, I think, are, like most white people, just as interested in maintaining their racial identity as most other peoples throughout the world. The real answer to that question depends on attitudes developed in the home, and on individual choice. There are not many interfaith marriages in this country, for obvious reasons, and I see no reason to expect that simply mixing the races in the schools would increase interracial marriage.

QUESTION: What about the effect on school standards of mixing in a high percentage of Negro children known to lag in scholastic achievement or aptitude?

ANSWER: Our own studies for the past decade show that the average Negro sixth-grader is a year and two months behind the average white sixth-grader in educational achievement. This lag exists in varying degrees at other levels, too, with the gap sometimes so great as to be almost alarming. This difference appears to be socio-economic rather than racial in basis. Records at the University of Louisville show, for instance, that Negroes who attended Central High School subsequently achieved at the University almost identically the same ratings they had at Central. If they barely squeaked through Central, they barely passed or failed at the University. If they were average at Central, they were average at the University. And, if they made excellent records at Central, they did the same at the University. In our city schools we propose to maintain, not lower, our standards when desegregation comes. It is going to be rugged, and our teachers' work-load will be heavy. I suspect that the percentage of non-promotions among Negro children will increase. But we will try to bring our mixed classes up to the same scholastic standard hitherto set in the all-white system. For these and other reasons the Negro children are the group for whom we need to have the greatest concern. Many of them will be under a distinct psychological handicap. It is the job of our schools to create that kind of climate in which they will have a minimum of insecurity and a maximum of feeling of belonging.

QUESTION: What about the teachers?

ANSWER: Sooner or later you are going to have Negro teachers teaching white children. That is what the Supreme Court decision means and that is what we will do. But mixing of races will not be pushed

63

abnormally for its own sake. There are some knotty problems ahead in this. For a variety of reasons, the average Negro teacher is less competent than the average white teacher. I can foresee that some Negro teachers of apparently superior training and experience may be passed over for white teachers seemingly less well-equipped. And it can happen that a white teacher from some influential family will lose out to a Negro of more ability when both seek the same job. It is going to be rugged, but as far as I can determine, the best teacher, Negro or white, is going to get the job. (This question is discussed more fully in a later chapter.)

QUESTION: What about disciplinary problems? We have enough white juvenile delinquents as it is without adding Negro delinquents to them.

ANSWER: There is little doubt that we must expect an increase in the number of minor incidents. Our purpose will be to make sure that they remain minor. Our standards of school discipline will not be lowered. We have a good police force, accustomed to dealing with white and Negro misconduct alike, and we can depend on them to keep minor troubles from becoming major troubles out in the community.

QUESTION: Can't we hope to keep some schools, at least, all-white?

ANSWER: Possibly a few, because of location, but not with any assurance that they will remain all-white indefinitely. We haven't worked out a detailed plan for desegregation yet, but the clear intent of the

Court will be applied. On the other hand, it is quite likely that a few Negro schools in the central part of the city will continue to be all-Negro simply because no white pupils live in their districts.

The Community in the Campaign

As I have indicated, our official emphasis was an appeal to that fundamental quality of good citizenship: recognition of the law and readiness to abide by it.

But we counted confidently on something of equal importance: the readiness of many citizens to be influenced by ethical, moral, religious or humanitarian considerations. And, perhaps, by the pragmatic lessons available from interracial experience in other fields.

We were not disappointed.

It was with the certainty of this in mind that I sought to enlist the support of every rabbi, minister and priest in Louisville. I sought the support officially, by letter, although fully aware that in many cases no request was necessary. The resulting contribution of religious leaders to the creation of a favorable climate was monumental. The attitude of the Catholic Church had long been opposed to racial segregation, and within months of the Supreme Court's decision, the highest representative bodies of virtually every major Protestant denomination had, in varying terms, identified the Court's ruling as in line with basic Christian doctrine.

Some of our local ministers prepared sermons vigorously supporting the principle of desegregation. Others told me privately they would defeat their own purposes by a frontal approach but said they would preach sermons on good human relations, touching guardedly and tactfully, if at all, on desegregation —and they did. Many arranged for study and discussion of desegregation by various groups in their churches.

Other elements of the community's leadership responded with equal vigor.

Here are some representative declarations by influential Louisvillians, and by some of their equally influential guests, during the campaign to create a climate of opinion favorable to change:

"No dispute on the University of Louisville campus has had a racial basis," President Philip Davidson told the Louisville Convention of the Southern Association of Colleges and Secondary Schools in December 1954. "Immediately after Negro students were first admitted, a lot of white students leaned over backward to have a Negro student on every committee, and things of that sort. But now student committees are picked on the basis of the best man for the job.

"We are not trying to promote racial equality or

social reform, but we are trying to offer a first-class educational institution in every way. We are building a solid experience that I hope will be of value to the rest of you."

Jefferson County School Superintendent Van Hoose, whose system fortunately was developing a program not dissimilar to the city's, said in the same month:

"I do not anticipate any serious racial trouble regardless of the way we are told to integrate. I hope the Supreme Court will give us a little time to put desegregation into action. It is not a matter of racial conflict, but rather a matter of housing."

Russell Sexton, an Ahrens High School student, on an interracial panel at his white high school—one of many similar forums sponsored by various organizations:

"The main cause of friction between Negroes and whites is prejudice. We have to educate adults and parents to see that it is right to have Negroes and whites in the same classrooms."

Mary Perry, Central High student, on the same forum:

"Segregation is contrary to the Constitution and hinders the economic, social and educational development of the individual. It results in unequal expenditure for Negro and white schools."

Robert L. Carter, New York attorney for the National Association for the Advancement of Colored

People, at an interracial seminar sponsored by the Southern Police Institute at the University of Louisville:

"The Supreme Court has now said that equality under the law means equality in fact . . . this is the beauty of the decision. Morality and equality have merged as one and that, I believe, constitutes an irresistible force."

A conclusion reached by white and Negro students from eighteen colleges at a 1955 meeting in Louisville during Brotherhood Week, sponsored by the National Conference of Christians and Jews:

"Prejudice begins at home. Many racial and religious hatreds that have no basis in fact today exist because they have been handed down from generation to generation. Young people must recognize this and base their opinions upon their own experience. And, when they become parents, they must be careful not to influence the opinions of their own children."

Mrs. James Tate, President of "Youth Speaks," at an interracial program before the Kentucky Congress of Colored Parents and Teachers, in May 1955:

"I hope that integration will be accomplished not only as integration but as integration with friendship."

The *Courier-Journal* in June 1955, commenting on action in Frankfort:

"The State Board of Education is to be commended for urging local school authorities to begin integration of white and Negro pupils 'as rapidly as possible.' For while it acted with common sense and in clear accord with the spirit of the Supreme Court ruling, these qualities have not yet been evinced by a large number of other state boards.

"The board's major recommendation, it is true, might well have been made earlier. But it still puts Kentucky in the vanguard of those states committed to sensible and orderly compliance with the Supreme Court's ruling, and it is fully in line with Governor Wetherby's promise last year and this that Kentucky would do whatever the law required.

"Chairman Wendell P. Butler, the State Superintendent of Public Instruction, and his board may well feel that they have met the challenge of duty."

Dr. Ralph J. Bunche, Under Secretary General of the United Nations, at the January 1956 Brotherhood Awards Dinner of the Kentucky Region of the National Conference of Christians and Jews:

"Democracy is weakened by segregation . . . Louisville's program in race relations shows that fears about desegregation quickly explode when a community summons courage to take moderately bold steps."

The Rev. Ralph Galloway, a missionary to the French Cameroons, in a 1956 Louisville Presbyterian Seminary lecture:

"The missionary, whose first duty is to preach the gospel of Jesus Christ, is doing what he can to combat Communistic propaganda—but many times what we do and say is compromised by what is being done in the Southern United States and elsewhere."

State Superintendent of Public Instruction Robert Martin, at the 80th annual session of the Kentucky Teachers Association (Negro) in Louisville in April 1956:

"Integration in Kentucky schools has progressed without incident and without the mouthings of demagogues. . . . I would be less than honest if I did not admit that the integration of teachers will present a much bigger problem than the integration of children. I don't believe the problem is insurmountable. But you must insist on your rights as teachers and human beings."

A spokesman for Archbishop John A. Floersch, commenting on the fact that a few Catholic schools had accepted Negroes in 1955 and that three Catholic high schools would enroll them in 1956:

"The announcement that Catholic schools are to be integrated is unnecessary. The Church's policy is one of no distinction and no segregation. Catholic schools would have accepted Negroes long ago, as several colleges have been doing since 1950, if the Day Law had not made this illegal."

A Speech in Florida

And here are some highlights of what the publisher of the *Courier-Journal* and the *Louisville*

Times, Mark F. Ethridge, said in a speech to University of Florida journalism students on February 20, 1956:

"Desegregation, integration—call it what you will —hangs like a dark cloud over the South and no editor can dare ignore it as a major editorial problem. . . .

"Now, nobody desires to hurry the transition which the Supreme Court decreed to be the law of the land, which our intelligence told us was inevitable, which our conscience told us was right. Nor has the Supreme Court insisted upon a hurried transition. It has given the seventeen states affected a 'reasonable time' and, moreover, it returned enforcement to the local courts, knowing that special problems are presented where the population is overwhelmingly Negro. . . .

"It is easier to lynch mentally the N.A.A.C.P. than to face the hard facts. I must in candor say that the N.A.A.C.P. is vulnerable to attack. It is not one of my favorite organizations. It is sometimes as radical on its side as Senator Eastland is on his. By trying to hurry too fast, it can violate the spirit if not the word of the Supreme Court decision quite as grossly as Senator Eastland in trying to defeat it. . . .

"The reasonable people of the South are caught between two forces: one of them sitting down in the traces like a balky mule, the other trying to move it by setting firecrackers under its belly.

"Both attitudes are dangerous.

"But, when all that has been said, it must be repeated that there are hard facts to be faced by calm and sober people—facts not advanced by political demagogues or agitators.

"One of them is that the South will not be allowed to withdraw from the Union; it will not be allowed to establish defiance of the Supreme Court as the law of the land; it will not be allowed to bend the will of the Union to denial of the civil rights or full citizenship of a tenth of our population any more than it was allowed to continue to enslave that minority. It will not profit by attempts at slick evasion even though it may long delay integration. . . .

"Not since the Civil War has the Southern editor faced such a challenge as he has now to fight the blackheartedness of organized prejudice and repression and fanaticism on the one hand and give calm counsel on the other to people who believe in living under the law and in expanding the freedoms of all of us."

A Sermon on the Church and Segregation

I have already commented on the contribution of Louisville's religious leaders to the creation of a climate of opinion favorable to school desegregation. It is not feasible, of course, to quote at length from many of the sermons that were preached. But I know of no more fitting way to end this chapter than by

citing one representative sermon. It was delivered
on December 12, 1954, by Dr. William A. Benfield,
Jr., in the Highland Presbyterian Church.

A graduate of North Carolina's Davidson College
(and recipient of Davidson's honorary Doctor of Di-
vinity degree), Dr. Benfield has lived in Louisville
since 1938. He took his theological training at the
105-year-old Louisville Presbyterian Seminary, later
served as the Seminary's vice-president and professor
of practical theology before accepting the Highland
pastorate in 1949.

The particular denomination to which he refers in
the following excerpts is, of course, the Presbyterian
Church of the United States (Southern):

"During the latter part of World War II the grad-
uating class of a certain high school was assigned as
the subject for a composition, 'What Just Punishment
Should Be Meted Out to Adolf Hitler?' A Negro girl
won the prize by developing the thesis that he should
be put into a black skin and set down in the midst of
a white community.

"The story is a parable on the history of these
United States of America—a parable which many of
us do not like to hear and for which we all should
hang our heads in shame. . . .

"Last year the Council of Christian Relations of
our Presbyterian denomination was asked to study
the matter of segregation in church-controlled institutions and report to the next General Assembly. The

report of this Council was adopted with (among others) the following recommendation:

" 'That the General Assembly affirm that enforced segregation of the races is discrimination which is out of harmony with Christian theology and ethics and that the church, in its relationship to cultural patterns, should lead rather than follow . . .'

"It is in light of this action of the highest court of our church that I ask you to think with me this morning about the church and segregation. I am aware that some of you are not going to concur completely with what is now to be said, and this is of course your right and privilege under the freedom of conscience which we enjoy in our Protestant tradition. Perhaps no one of us with white skin realizes the sharpness of the issue before us . . .

"As a professing Christian, I am both proud and ashamed of the action which my denomination has taken through its highest body of representative officers. I am proud because I believe this action to be in accord with the teachings of the Bible and the teachings of Christ. I am ashamed because this action has been so long delayed and comes as the consequence of many secular movements instead of being the motivating force behind such movements . . .

"Some forty million people in our country today suffer from some kind of discrimination, and the largest group is the Negro. In nearly every state in which our particular Presbyterian denomination is at work there are laws which segregate Negroes and whites,

74

in schools, in modes of transportation, in waiting
rooms, in public meeting places, in centers of amuse-
ment, in hospitals, in institutions of social and penal
correction. And in the states of our nation where
such laws do not exist, the attitude and action of the
white citizenry make segregation a continued reality.

"For the creation and maintenance of this dark picture the Christian church itself must wear the badge
of infamy. Segregation in the secular areas has been
and is being supported by Christian people. The
Christian church has practiced and is practicing segregation in its own programs . . .

"It is here, in the matter of Christian teachings
and Christian influence, that I want now to say something positive about the church and segregation. Our
General Assembly has affirmed that enforced segregation of the races is discrimination which is out of
harmony with Christian theology and ethics and that
the church, in its relationship to cultural patterns,
should lead rather than follow. This affirmation I accept without qualification and I pray that you, my
fellow Christians, will accept it also.

"In the first place I urge the adoption of this position in your own Christian commitment because of
the teaching of the Holy Word of God regarding the
nature of man. There are times when we all hesitate
to think deeply about race relations because we know
that an open, frank consideration will cut right across
our deep-rooted prejudices and our smug compla-
cency. But as Christians there is one, and always

75

only one, basic standard for our beliefs and our actions. This is the Word of God, the only infallible rule of faith and practice.

"There are earnest Christians who have a particular view of the nature and worth and status of the Negro as a human being. The view holds that Negroes, though truly human and members of the family of God, are nonetheless inferior beings who belong to an innately inferior race. But the belief that some people are inferior to others because of race or ancestry is nowhere supported by the Bible. The idea is never taught by Christ or Paul or any of the great fathers of the church. The truth of the matter is that the doctrine of Negro inferiority is a secular idea . . .

"The idea that one branch of the human family is inferior to the others, or, conversely, that one particular branch is inherently superior to the others, is not supported by scientific fact. As one American anthropologist put it, 'There are only superior individuals, and they are members of all races.' The Bible teaches that every person is of infinite value, and therefore of equal value in the sight of God. In His sight there is no superior race . . .

"And this leads to the second thing to be said. Divisions among men are not native to man but are the result of human sin. And it was precisely to restore the unity of mankind in the family of God that He came to earth. As Christians we have no differences of race or color. As Christians we are not Negroes and whites, Americans and Japanese—we are sons of God, people made in the image of God who were separated, divided by the will of man, and who now through the indwelling of Christ are united through the love which God has for us all.

"And here let me say a word about a concern which many earnest Christians have. There are those who recognize that segregation and Christian idealism cannot be reconciled but who are afraid that with the disappearance of segregation Southern white people will be forced against their will to accept as social intimates or companions persons whose fellowship at this level they do not desire, and will lead to widespread intermarriage. For one thing it should be said that most Negroes frown upon intermarriage just as severely as we do. It should also be recognized that in the states where non-segregation policies are in effect, racial intermarriage does not occur frequently. In one of our largest cities, for example, there has been a steady decrease in Negro-white marriages since 1914. But most significant of all, it should be pointed out that the abolishment of segregation does not mean we shall no longer be free to choose our friends and associates. No person of feeling wants to be compelled to do otherwise, and any social arrangement that violates the individual's right to personal privacy would be unjust and offensive to Negroes and whites alike. In the same manner in which we are free to choose our friends we would also be free to choose our husbands and wives. The matter of selecting the right marital partner is not one of segregation or non-segregation . . .

"We are entering a new era in race relationships in

our nation. Of this there is no question. The big question has to do with the quality of these relationships and it is here that we of the church must speak and act and live. Many serious issues are going to be met and resolved, in one way or another, here in our own city and throughout the Southland. We have the Gospel of Jesus Christ as the answer, and thus it is that I challenge you this morning to rethink your own position as a believer in Him who came to bring peace and joy to all men.

"If you believe in racial segregation, it is your privilege to so believe. But you must be prepared to answer for your position some day to Him who said, 'Inasmuch as you have done it unto one of the least of these, my brothers, you have done it unto me.'

"If you do not believe in racial segregation, then it is time for you to do something about it, and there is much you can do. You can take advantage of every opportunity to correct fake ideas, fears and misunderstandings about the Negro race and the implications of a non-segregated society. You can give active support to the educational and civic endeavors of our community in race relations. You can give support to the Christian churches which should and will open their doors of membership to people of any race who profess faith in the Lord Jesus Christ. And above all you can in your personal relationships with your fellow-men manifest the love of God who is no respecter of persons. . . ."

► v ◄

△

The Louisville Plan:
To Break the Ice

THE FULL YEAR spent in study and community discussion, before any effort was made to begin to develop a plan, had some important advantages. It enabled the faculties of each school to discover, analyze and clearly state all the problems and questions which they thought should have consideration in the final development of an over-all plan for desegregation.

There was also, naturally, both in and out of the schools, much informal discussion of possible solutions of the various problems defined. The lack of haste and the absence of any deadline pressure contributed a great deal to the calmness of such discussions.

It was on May 31, 1955, that the Supreme Court handed down its second ruling on school desegregation.

The next day the *Courier-Journal* summed up much local reaction in this editorial comment:

"The Supreme Court has sensibly undertaken to set no deadline, and has left with the Federal District Courts the determination whether 'action of school authorities constitutes good faith implementation of the governing constitutional principles.'

"These principles are perfectly clear. A citizen is a citizen whether rich or poor, black or white. He deserves the same protection under the law as his fellow; his children deserve the same education in the same tax-supported school system as the children of his neighbors. As the Supreme Court remarked: 'validity of these constitutional principles can not be allowed to yield simply because of disagreement with them.' "

The same day as the Court's ruling, in a newspaper interview, I made these points:

"The Louisville Board of Education had accepted the principle of the original Court decision a full year before.

"Now that the Court's final decision has been made, we can go to work to develop a plan.

"This will include redistricting where necessary to better utilize school buildings, deciding whether to let children transfer from one school to another freely or sparingly, deciding whether to introduce integration throughout the system at once, or in certain geographic areas, or by grades.

"I favor starting integration only at the beginning of a school year and not during the term. I believe another year of general background building, interpreting, and getting people to understand, is needed. It is a big order for a year, but I think you can spend too long on a thing and I have no desire to want to slow down."

Board President Morton Walker at the same time publicly stated his belief that September 1956 would be the time to begin integration in Louisville.

One week later—at the first board meeting following the Court's action—I submitted two memorandums. One reviewed the history of the school year just ending. The other made these proposals:

(1) that I present, no later than mid-November of 1955, at least a tentative plan for integration, and

(2) the general integration studies initiated the year before be continued in 1955–1956.

The Board of Education unanimously endorsed both of these proposals.

On June 23, the State Board of Education, which a year earlier had advised maintenance of the status quo, officially urged local school authorities to begin integration "as rapidly as conditions warrant."

On June 27 the Jefferson County Board of Education took action comparable to that of the Louisville Board and set the same target date for integration—a fortunate development in assuring simultaneous action by school authorities throughout the greater Louisville area. The county schools had fewer than 1,000 Negro pupils in a total enrollment of 33,000, but experience in other communities had suggested the wisdom of a common and simultaneous approach toward desegregation in city and suburban areas alike.

Our target date of 1956 did not escape some criticism. At a local N.A.A.C.P. meeting some speakers accused us of stalling. But a suggestion from the floor that the N.A.A.C.P. seek legal action to force integration that fall did not come to a vote. The majority accepted the warning of Attorney Harry McAlpin that "we might get tangled up in legal matters that might hold up integration for some time after 1956." The group, instead, instructed its education committee to put forth every effort to aid the Board of Education to complete integration in 1956.

During the next few months our administrative and supervisory staff worked overtime preparing the plan for submission in November.

Copies of the plan were sent to all schools and Parent-Teacher Association presidents and published in the local newspapers with the request that any organization or individual submit in writing any suggestions for improvement. When only one suggestion had been received and that for a very minor change, the Board of Education at its December 1955 meeting adopted the plan as submitted and the staff went to work to carry it out.

In the preparation of the plan, we spent a great deal of time weighing the relative merits of a gradual change to be accomplished in a few years, against those of a system-wide change wholly effective from the beginning.

We decided on a simultaneous system-wide change. There were several reasons for this. Experience elsewhere indicated that a partial or geographic change particularly might lead to mushrooming opposition. Desegregating a grade at a time or several grades at a time obviously would increase social confusion by having some children in a single family attend mixed schools while others remained in segregated schools. Administrative difficulties, too, obviously would be compounded by any partial program. And we decided that universality of participation by the entire school staff from the very beginning would greatly increase the chances of success.

Our first step was to redistrict the entire school system—first for elementary schools and then for junior high schools—without regard to race, and with no gerrymandering. Redistricting was an obvious necessity, since only so many pupils could be assigned to the one school in each district, and with the abolition of the old dual system, that one school must accommodate pupils of all races.

The Louisville Plan

Here are the twelve points of the desegregation plan adopted by the Board of Education (nine months before it was to be put into effect):

1. The program shall go into operation in September 1956.

2. The change shall be complete—throughout the Louisville School District and at all levels, kindergarten through high school and adult classes.

3. The entire area of the Louisville School District will be redistricted without regard to race.

4. In redistricting, there shall be no gerrymandering or other establishment of unnatural boundaries.

5. The redistricting shall be done in such manner as to serve all the children as conveniently as possible, with proper regard to the capacities of buildings.

6. To each school shall be assigned an area which will furnish, without excessive travel, the approximate number of pupils, regardless of race, which it may reasonably serve.

7. If two or more schools are close together, or for other reasons it seems wise, a single district may be

established for them and parents may be permitted to choose freely between or among them within the capacities of the respective schools.

8. When new district lines have been established and approved by the Board of Education, parents of all children will be informed in writing of the school or schools in which their children belong.

9. A parent who prefers another school may request a transfer. The transfer and the parent's preference of schools will be granted within the capacities of the schools and with due regard for the convenience of the child and the preferences and conveniences of other parents and children.

10. Transfers such as those described in paragraph 9 above shall not be permitted to crowd out of any school pupils who, by residence, belong in the school.

11. A pupil attending a school other than the one which serves the district in which he lives may be required to transfer to the school in which he belongs by residence if attendance, conduct or school work is not satisfactory.

12. Pupils attending a school outside the district of residence will not receive free transportation, except in unusual cases which the superintendent may approve.

The most notable feature of this plan, aside perhaps from its simplicity, is its free choice or permissive aspect. No redistricting was necessary for the six senior high schools. Thanks to the possibility of free-choice transfers to everyone, there could be no assurance that a single school anywhere in the city would remain segregated.

We saw the permissive feature in the first year of integration as a good ice-breaker certain to minimize individual opposition to the plan. We believed, and subsequent events justified that belief, that a good many parents of both races, particularly in the beginning, would prefer their children to attend schools in which their own race was not a small minority.

There was again some criticism from N.A.A.C.P. spokesmen of the free-choice aspect of the plan. But the local branch endorsed it as "basically very good."

To Mrs. Zimmerman, the P.T.A. Council president, the flexible feature seemed "a good safety valve." Charlton Hummel, president of the Louisville Education Association, termed it the proper approach: "It will create the least friction. There will be administrative problems, but there will be fewer problems than if a tight system were adopted." And the local newspapers editorially agreed that, administered in good faith, the plan could fully match the letter and the spirit of the Supreme Court ruling and "achieve a momentous change with a minimum of friction."

When redistricting was completed—on the strictest basis of school capacity and population distribution— a card (reproduced on page 87) was sent to the parents of each elementary and each junior high-school pupil, telling them the school to which their

CARD USED IN LOUISVILLE 'FREE CHOICE' PLAN

Dear Parent:

On the reverse side of this card is the plan adopted by the Board of Education for ending compulsory racial segregation in the Louisville Public Schools. In the redistricting, your child

_____   _____
Pupil's Name   (First)   (Last)   Address

_____   _____
(Present School)   (Present Grade)

belongs in _____ school.

If you prefer another school, please list below your 1st, 2nd, and 3rd choice and return to the school your child is now attending on or before March 8, 1956. When there are more requests for transfers than can be granted, decisions will be made in accordance with items 9 and 10 of the plan.

First   Second   Third
Choice_____   Choice_____   Choice_____

PARENT PLEASE SIGN AND RETURN _____
                                       Signature of Parent or Guardian

PLAN OF THE BOARD OF EDUCATION FOR DESEGREGATION

1. The program shall go into operation in September, 1956.
2. The change shall be complete—throughout the Louisville School District and at all levels, kindergarten through high school and adult classes.
3. The entire area of the Louisville School District will be redistricted without regard to race.
4. In redistricting, there shall be no gerrymandering or other establishment of unnatural boundaries.
5. The redistricting shall be done in such manner as to serve all the children as conveniently as possible, with proper regard to the capacities of buildings.
6. To each school shall be assigned an area which will furnish, without excessive travel, the approximate number of pupils, regardless of race, which it may reasonably serve.
7. If two or more schools are close together, or for other reasons it seems wise, a single district may be established for them and parents may be permitted to choose freely between or among them within the capacities of the respective schools.
8. When new district lines have been established and approved by the Board of Education, parents of all children will be informed in writing the school or schools in which their children belong.
9. A parent who prefers another school may request a transfer. The transfer and the parent's preference of schools will be granted within the capacities of the schools and with due regard for the convenience of the child and the preferences and convenience of other parents and children.
10. Transfers such as those described in paragraph 9 above shall not be permitted to crowd out of any school pupils who, by residence, belong in this school.
11. A pupil attending a school other than the one which serves the district in which he lives may be required to transfer to the school in which he belongs by residence if attendance, conduct or school work is not satisfactory.
12. Pupils attending a school outside the district of residence will not receive free transportation, except in unusual cases which the superintendent may approve.

ABOVE is a reproduction of the card sent to parents and guardians of nearly 50,000 Louisville school children in the winter and spring of 1956. Replies were used in working out the flexible-transfer program under which pupils were assigned to individual schools.

child was assigned. The card also told the parents, if they preferred another school, to indicate first, second and third choices. Each parent was assured that transfer requests would be granted and the choice of schools respected, subject only to the capacities of the individual school building. On the reverse side of the card, which every parent was asked to sign and return, the entire twelve-point plan was reproduced for easy consultation.

Numbers alone will indicate the vast administrative and clerical labor needed to accommodate transfer requests and tabulate acceptances from the parents of some 41,762 elementary and junior high-school children.

Of that number some 37,247, or 89 per cent, accepted the schools to which their children had been assigned under redistricting. Some 4,515, or 11 per cent, requested transfers.

There were some interesting patterns in the transfer requests. Of Negro children assigned to what had been white schools, the parents of 45 per cent requested transfers back to what had been Negro schools. Of white children assigned by redistricting to what had been Negro schools, the parents of 85 per cent requested transfers.

Of all the requested transfers, 90 per cent got their first choices. Most of the other 10 per cent got their second or third choice. There were very few who could get no one of their choices because the buildings they preferred were filled—and this led to patient conferences with the more disgruntled parents before they were led to accept what had to be.

When all the requests for transfers had been processed, another card was sent to all parents, not just those requesting transfers, explaining what had been done, expressing regret that there were a few who could not have their first choices, thanking them all for their past and what we were sure would be their future co-operation, and telling them the school to which their child would report in September.

There was no redistricting, as I observed earlier, for the senior high schools. A card was sent to parents of all pupils announcing that each senior high school was open to pupils of both races who lived in the district which it served, and that transfers to others would be possible. Because the Negro senior high school, Central, has the newest and best plant in the city, and because an excellent faculty has created a fine school loyalty among the students, there were almost no transfers from it to what had been the five all-white senior high schools—despite the fact that for many Negro pupils some of the latter would have been much more convenient. Approximately 100 tenth-grade Negro pupils, promoted from the ninth grade of junior high schools, chose the geographically more convenient white senior high schools rather than Central.

We knew that there were many individual citizens not happy about the plan for desegregation—my assistants and I had conferences enough with them.

But most of them generally eased whatever their objections were by requesting transfers for their children to schools where they hoped there would be few or no members of the other race.

There was no evidence of organized opposition to the program until the spring of 1956, when a white Citizens Council for Kentucky was chartered. Its local branch did not attract much numerical support. Meetings in the late spring and early summer seldom found more than twenty-five or thirty people attending. An intensified campaign in late summer built attendance up to a little less than 100, but by September attendance was diminishing.

This organization was responsible for a petition in August to the Board of Education. Signed by eighty persons and presented by about twenty, it held that mixing Negro and white children in the schools was a violation of state law, that 85 per cent of Kentucky parents opposed it and that the Supreme Court had no authority to order desegregation. The document added: "We will do everything in our power to prevent you from violating the law of the state, and we will not allow our children to attend any schools where both white and Negro children are enrolled."

At the board meeting, I told the petitioners that the Louisville program was developed on a gradual, considerate basis, and cautioned the petitioners against making it hard for themselves and others and making the children innocent sufferers.

Board President Keith C. Spears gave the delegation the final answer: "The Supreme Court has handed down the decision and we are going to integrate this fall."

When one woman in the delegation insisted that "good white people should not allow this sort of thing," Board Member Yancey R. Altsheler retorted: "We are good Americans first."

That was the way things stood in Louisville on the eve of the 1956–57 school year.

Other Developments

There were other developments in the 1954–56 period that directly affected the climate of opinion we were seeking in Louisville.

In early 1955, Jackie Robinson spoke at several interracial meetings in Louisville during Brotherhood Week. He was applauded. Nine years earlier, playing for Montreal against the Louisville Colonels of the American Association at Louisville's Parkway Field, he was booed every time he stepped to the plate and almost every time he made a move on the field. As sports writer Tommy Fitzgerald commented in his *Courier-Journal* column, the friendly applause accorded the Brooklyn star was in sharp contrast "with the wild, fierce winds of intolerance of 1946." Coupling this with the fact that "the Negro ballplayer is now accepted in Louisville," Fitzgerald commented that "considerable progress has been made toward a better brotherhood of man in just nine years."

In mid-1955 the State Board of Education, which a year earlier had advised maintenance of the status quo until the Supreme Court's second ruling, officially urged local school authorities to begin integration "as rapidly as conditions warrant."

Several Kentucky school systems initiated desegregation programs in 1955, and the state ended segregation in its three vocational schools and the state-operated School for the Blind. That school year found some 300 Kentucky Negroes in twenty-four school districts attending public schools with whites for the first time in the state's history.

Several more of the private or church-operated colleges also lowered their color bars during this period: twenty-eight of the state's forty institutions of higher learning, including junior colleges, were open to all races in 1956.

On September 29, 1955, the Louisville Education Association voted 246 to 18—binding on a membership of 1,214—to remove from its constitution a stipulation that all members be white and began accepting immediately the first of Louisville's 399 Negro teachers. (A much smaller organization, the Louisville Federation of Teachers, now claiming "two to four per cent" of the city's teachers, had been interracial from its beginning in 1941.)

The Kentucky Education Association quietly began

accepting Negro members in 1955 and in 1956. The state's teachers on May 26 agreed on "professional unification" of their separate organizations. The 79-year-old Kentucky Teachers Association (Negro), with some 1,500 members ceased to collect dues and encouraged its members to join the 20,000-member K.E.A., setting its formal dissolution for April 12, 1957.

In July of 1956 the Kentucky Department of the American Legion, in convention at Paducah, voted to erase the color bar in the annual "Boys State" program sponsored by the Legion to acquaint the youth of the state with governmental processes. The vote followed a report that white students chosen for the 1956 program had been polled and expressed no opposition to Negro participation.

In the same month, Louisville's racially separated Parent-Teacher Councils decided on a single inter-racial organization, and announced that local P.T.A.s would automatically be desegregated in the fall. The action merged a 50-year-old white council of 52 chapters and 28,000 members with a 5-year-old Negro council of 16 chapters and 3,000 members. Officers of the white council, elected earlier in the year for two-year terms, kept their positions in the combined organization—but members of the Negro executive board were appointed co-chairmen of nine council committees.

In that same July, Kentucky's Governor A. B. (Happy) Chandler, campaigning for the Democratic presidential nomination, restated his belief that "the Supreme Court is the Court of last resort and its decision is the law of the land."

And the two-year period saw an end to the long litigation involving racial segregation in the city parks and swimming pools. The Kentucky Court of Appeals late in 1955, citing a Supreme Court decision in a Maryland case, banned segregation in all public recreational facilities—parks, playgrounds and swimming pools—throughout the state.

Mayor Broaddus promptly declared that "we will observe the spirit as well as the letter of the decision" and disclosed that on his orders but without public announcement city police several months earlier had ceased to enforce park or playground segregation.

The Mayor said public announcement was withheld because "we wanted this change to grow gradually, and we were afraid such a pronouncement would bring about frictions." George Cordery, president of the Louisville branch of the N.A.A.C.P., said that it was a case simply of the Mayor having seen "the handwriting on the wall" and that City Hall was just going along because "it was futile to fight further." The issue dropped quietly out of the news.

In the summer of 1956 whites and Negroes for the first time shared the city's five public swimming pools —and without serious friction. Attendance dropped 30 per cent below the 1955 record—from 241,120 to 171,505. (Announcing these figures in November, Mayor Broaddus attributed the decline largely to an

unusually cool summer, and said that he did not believe desegregation was responsible.)

Also in that summer we jumped the gun on our
long-advertised schedule for desegregation, enrolling
twenty-eight Negroes among nearly 800 students at
the Louisville Summer High School. Principal Joe C.
Howard, with the pride of a pioneer, reported a
smooth operation.

The summer-school experiment, though it led to no
serious incidents, apparently intensified opposition
sentiment. Pranksters or more serious-minded persons burned wooden crosses on three school grounds
during the week of school registration (September
5–6). And there were fresh rumbles from white Citizens Council members and other opponents of integration.

We had long enjoyed the close co-operation of city
authorities and the police department. Now consul-
tations occurred more frequently with Chief of Police Carl Heustis and his aides in the Crime Prevention
Bureau. The same was true of Dick Van Hoose and
County Police Chief Walter Layman. And, since city
limits are no wall to trouble, city-county liaison was
close.

Long before the opening days of school—but without publicity—both police forces had completed their
trouble-prevention plans. The likelier trouble spots
were charted, special details (in uniform and out)
were assigned. Unmarked squad cars, with picked
personnel and two-way radios, would cruise unobtru-

sively but repeatedly past selected centers on Desegregation Day, in city and county alike. Long before D-Day, plain-clothes men would be mingling with potential trouble-makers like brothers, shadowing some who were heard to threaten violence, listening to the noise of what might come. And reporting.

It was from one of these that Chief Heustis learned, two days before a public announcement of it, that the white Citizens Council would picket the schools, in rotation, when school began. Their opening-day target: the system's oldest and most famous unit, coeducational now, but still glorying as it did on its founding exactly a century before in the title of Louisville Male High School.

When he heard that, Colonel Heustis canceled an engagement in Chicago. He decided that he would be at Male High himself on opening day. And early.

▶ **VI** ◀

△

The First Half-Year of
Transition

A *New Day in the Schools*

ON SEPTEMBER 10, 1956, I got up a little earlier than
usual. I thought I had better be at Male High
School too, to observe developments and to plan ac-
cordingly. I got there at 7:30.

Chief of Police Heustis was already there. His car,
with two-way radio and other officers, was parked a
few feet from the school entrance. And with him was
Director of Safety W. G. Matton.

Before any pupils arrived, the group assembled at Male included Mayor Broaddus, School Board President Spears, Assistant Superintendent W. F. Coslow, Male Principal W. S. Milburn—and a throng of reporters and photographers representing newspapers, news magazines, and radio and television stations, local and national. The preceding week had seen the outbreak of racial violence in several cities attempting desegregation, and the press was fully aware that Louisville was the largest city on their list of potential trouble spots.

But there was no trouble.

The pickets did not come. A White Citizens Council spokesman later explained that they had decided to picket the Board of Education building instead—because he could get no assurance from Commonwealth's Attorney A. Scott Hamilton that school pickets would not be arrested for creating "a clear and present danger." (And picket our offices they did, as well as the County School Board center two miles away, and City Hall. They picketed each for an hour or so, with large signs opposing "race mixing in the schools," "surrendering States' Rights to Communist-based Court opinion," and so on. But they attracted little attention—and, as the local newspapers reported, one was from Indiana, two or three from the suburbs, and not one was the parent of a Louisville school child.)

But we didn't know that no pickets were coming. And I must frankly admit that an air of uncertainty if not of apprehensive expectancy hovered around the entrance of Male High as the first of some 1,100 pupils began to enter.

The first pupils came singly or in small groups, some laughing and gay, some solemnly alert or inquisitive, all, in their youth, so warming to the heart. Most of them went promptly into the building, but a few lingered outside.

There were perhaps 200 still outside on the school grounds at 8:20, ten minutes before classes were to begin. Photographers were busily taking pictures and reporters were interviewing pupils at random. Such activities, coupled with the presence of city notables not normally present on opening day, might reasonably have caused more than the normal congregation of pupils. At that, the throng remaining outside was not much larger than would be expected on the first day of school. The one big difference was that some were Negroes, some were white. And all were orderly.

But about 8:20 Chief Heustis asked if I didn't think he should order the pupils to go into the building. I replied that such a preschool gathering was natural, the group was well-behaved and the warning bell would ring in a few minutes. It seemed better to me to have everything go along naturally if possible.

Five minutes later the warning bell rang. And all the students, white and Negro, went into the building as on any other opening day.

It was a good beginning.

It was much the same in all of the city's seventy-five public schools that day.

Police in their patrol cars cruised past possible trouble spots, as planned, throughout that historic Monday. And some 500 officers were available on call.

But it was a quiet day in Louisville.

As Benjamin Fine reported in *The New York Times* the following morning:

"White and Negro children rushed through the school corridors together. They solemnly recited the Pledge of Allegiance in unison. Pupils sat side by side in the classrooms. And they rushed gaily down the school steps together when the first day had ended. Color differences seemed forgotten.

"When the history of this proud Southern city is written, this day will undoubtedly go down as an historic landmark. Historians will note that a social revolution took place that may advance the cause of integration by a generation. Even in the South, it was shown here, integration can be made to work without violence."

Newspapers around the country carried many a report on how pupils and teachers adjusted to the change. There was a rash of "discoveries," among both races, that people are people, after all.

Miss Freda Zuercher, of the DuPont Manual High School faculty, pretty well summed it up for many. A veteran of some forty years in the city schools, she found herself for the first time teaching about thirty Negroes in her five English classes.

"I thought it might bother me, but it doesn't one bit," she said. "The children act as though they had been going to school with colored pupils all their lives. I think it is marvelous. I really can't understand it. But I like it."

We were just beginning our program. We had ended the first day of school with 73.6 per cent of all our pupils for the first time enrolled in racially mixed student bodies. Nobody knew what lay ahead. But Mayor Broaddus made a prophetic comment:

"I think the people of Louisville," he said, "are broad-minded enough to accept the situation as it is."

Some Unexpected Bouquets

We had begun our program even more smoothly than I had dared hope. Apparently the smoothness surprised and pleased a good many people far beyond Louisville, including President Eisenhower.

Anyone can imagine the pleasure and astonishment with which I read the remarks of Mr. Eisenhower at his Washington press conference on September 11.

The President commented on the great quiet in the Louisville schools and added:

"I think Mr. Carmichael must be a very wise man. I hope to meet him and I hope to get some advice from him as to exactly how he did it, because he pursued the policy that I believe will finally bring success in this."

In newspaper interviews later that day, I said that of course it was a matter of pride to a superintendent and to a community that what had been done seemed to merit comment from such a high source. But I added:

"If there is merit in what we are doing, the publicity incidental to it gives that much more value in spreading it to other communities.

"The whole thing is no individual achievement. It represents teamwork within the school system and a school-community relationship capable of developing a climate of public opinion in which a program can succeed."

Subsequently I was honored by an invitation to the White House and on September 20 I arrived for a half-hour appointment with the President.

It was an easy and informal conference. The President asked a good many questions—which indicated a deep interest and an understanding of some of the problems involved—and the appointment ran overtime some fifteen minutes. The answers I gave to the Presidential questions, as you might well surmise, are pretty well covered in the foregoing pages. At the conclusion, Mr. Eisenhower restated his belief that the thorough preparation made in Louisville, on a community-wide basis, is the pattern which can bring success in other areas.

It was a natural consequence of such attention from

the White House, I have since been told, that I suddenly found myself in great demand for a variety of public appearances, magazine interviews, "Voice of America" broadcasts, and national television programs.

As a seasoned schoolman, I derived a certain amount of gratification from all this and from some of the resultant bouquets. I was particularly glad that the Louisville experiment seemed to merit such wide publicity. But I regretted that such focusing of the national spotlight on an individual inevitably minimized what was, as I hope these pages show, a community achievement in which not merely hundreds but thousands of persons participated and in which their efforts would have come to naught had it not been for the firm foundation of the respect of Louisville citizens for law and order and their recognition of the human rights involved.

For this reason, I think that of all of the things written about the Louisville program, I like best the following editorial from *The New York Times*. It, too, exaggerated the role of a single man in a community enterprise. But it did give Louisville its due as a city:

Louisville's Good Example

Louisville is a city of many claims to fame, but no achievement so well commands the quiet satisfaction of a job well done as the orderly unexcited acceptance of desegregation within the public schools that took place there.

The largest Kentucky city, and the largest in the South to comply substantially with the Supreme Court's order as to Negro children, Louisville demonstrated the wisdom of complete preparation. The Superintendent of Schools, Dr. Omer Carmichael, was Alabama born. His life has been spent in the South. He has reason to say that he thinks he understands how the South feels about segregation. But he says, "we should have long-range plans to comply with the Supreme Court order, rather than to oppose it."

There were some aspects of speed, some of deliberation in Dr. Carmichael's program. He took the public into his confidence. He co-operated as far as possible with parents who wished to transfer their children, as he reorganized school districts. Some all-Negro schools remain, some all-white; some classes in other schools have only one per cent Negroes, others as high as forty-two per cent in predominantly white schools. In some other schools white children will be outnumbered by Negroes.

For two years the Superintendent has been laying the groundwork, in speeches and meetings, for peaceful compliance. Yesterday as schools opened there were no mobs, no pickets, no need for calling the Guard to put out fires. The people of Louisville proved once again that theirs is an enlightened, civilized city, revering a great past but ready to move on with the times.

Some Minor Headaches

The first half-year of transition was not all smooth sailing. There were some headaches. And some of them used up countless hours of administrative time. But fortunately the headaches all were minor.

First of all, naturally, the flexible transfer system took its toll of man-hours. This problem had been solved, at least on paper, back in the spring. But the thunder of trouble in other cities the week before the Louisville schools opened had two almost predictable results: a few score parents who had approved their children's school placement in the spring belatedly sought (and got) transfers, and a very few others decided to "wait and see" before sending their children to school at all.

Some of the former, despite the full publicity accorded our whole program, were pleasantly surprised to learn that their children could be transferred to schools of the parents' choice. It was not unamusing to see how quickly some attitudes of hot belligerence then changed to relieved acceptance of proffered alternatives—but it was convincing evidence that the free-choice feature, though from the beginning it could guarantee no one attendance in a segregated school, eased the road to change for many a dubious parent.

In the wait-and-see cases all of these were resolved fairly promptly. Attendance officers reminded tardy parents of the Kentucky law requiring all children under sixteen to attend school, and usually that was sufficient.

But there was one case not of wait-and-see but of a determined "never." The mother in question (I see no point in naming her) at the beginning of the school year, following a conference with Juvenile Court authorities, transferred her two teen-age children from a racially mixed junior high to the only one in the city having no Negro pupils—and when that one in December acquired its first and only Negro pupil, she withdrew her children with the announcement that they would never be allowed to attend school with Negroes.

I spent several long conferences with this mother, hopeful that I could change her mind without having to invoke the law. Among other things I pointed out that she was making her children the innocent victims of her determination by depriving them of their schooling.

But she was adamant, and reluctantly we resorted to the law. In January she and her husband, an elevator operator, were charged with contributing to the neglect and delinquency of their two oldest children by "wilfully failing to provide proper schooling or any schooling for them since December 13."

"I'll go to jail," the mother said, "but I won't let them force me to send my children to school with Negroes."

"It's not a question of integration," said Assistant County Attorney James E. Thornberry. "It's a question of these people not having their children in school."

At the first Juvenile Court hearing the mother told Judge Louis Jull that she planned to enroll the children in Portland Christian School, a private school supported by contributions from Churches of Christ and by tuition fees.

But Portland Christian Principal Claude Neal refused to admit the children—"because," he said, "we
are too crowded now and because we don't exist for
the purpose of taking in children whose parents don't
want them to attend school with Negroes." (No Negroes had sought admission to the church school, Neal
said, and the school's board had not ruled one way or
another on admitting them.)

With that the father of the children decided at last
to enroll them at Eastern Junior High, the school from
which they had first transferred in September (785
white pupils, 70 Negroes). The mother in public statements made it plain that the decision was not hers—
but she went along with it. "Anything they do from
now on," she said, "is their business. They can stay out
till twelve at night or four in the morning. Let the
Court raise them. I'll give them a place to sleep and
something to eat."

The mother has at least one consolation—and by
now, I devoutly hope, more. She had been paying a
relatively hard price in dollars for her convictions.
Now it no longer costs her two dollars a week to send
the children by bus to a distant school.

It was pleasantly surprising that no more cases like
this developed. For several weeks, during which similar tactics achieved considerable success in three Kentucky communities and in Clinton, Tennessee, opponents of desegregation conducted a fairly well organized telephone campaign to induce a boycott of
mixed classes.

Callers in some cases identified themselves as mem-

bers of the White Citizens Councils of Kentucky. They
shifted their attack from school to school. Some of the
calls were abusive or threatening (as had been a
few letters, over the months, to me and to other school
officials—letters we hopefully ascribed to non-danger-
ous cranks, and hence ignored).

But the campaign never caught on.

The Branham Case

On the whole, as a matter of fact, we have been unusually free from either local or outside interference
in our desegregation program. The principal exception
to this is a series of enlightening incidents centering
around Billy Branham, a seventeen-year-old Detroit
high school senior who had attended elementary
schools in his native eastern Kentucky.

Branham came to Louisville from Detroit sometime
in November, took a room at the YMCA, spent several days "visiting around" several of the senior high
schools, and told numerous students of his plans to organize opposition to desegregation. At Male High he
invited several students to come to his room at the
Y to discuss his plans, including the possible picket-
ing of Male.

When Male Principal Milburn learned of this,
he asked the police department to investigate Branham and his activities. The detective who interviewed

Branham got a gift of a collection of anti-integration literature from the youngster, the offer of more, and a full discussion of his intentions. Among them: a possible "strike" against integration.

The police advised Branham that he would be arrested if he violated any laws. But they gave him a clean bill in their report: he had not committed any seditious act or incited anyone toward riot.

Because of his subsequent rapid identification with the white Citizens Councils of Kentucky, Branham was thought by some to be a very special "import." But apparently he was not: soon after his arrival he went to the information office of the local newspapers to get the names and addresses of Council leaders.

After the Thanksgiving holidays Branham applied for admission to Male High. Because of his earlier activities, the application was referred to Assistant Superintendent Coslow for determination of Branham's residential status.

Mr. Coslow deferred action until my return to the city twenty-four hours later, when he and I had a two-hour conference with Billy.

I have to admit that he did most of the talking. He reaffirmed in considerable detail his purpose to agitate against our desegregation program—and insisted that the school system had no jurisdiction over out-of-school conduct.

We told him that in Louisville we do assume jurisdiction over out-of-school conduct of pupils when, in our judgment, the circumstances require. And we said we would have to consider information from Detroit before we could decide the following day on his residential status.

Billy told us that his mother was renting an apartment at 1427 South Sixth Street (which happens to be the home of Millard D. Grubbs, chairman of the white Citizens Councils of Kentucky, Inc.), that she had returned temporarily to Detroit but would return to Louisville with her husband, a welder, when they disposed of the four-family apartment house they owned there.

The Detroit report rated Billy as a student with some leadership qualities who had done satisfactory classroom work in the ninth, tenth, and eleventh grades there. It described his record as a school citizen as satisfactory, despite a display of "some poor judgment" in connection with a debate in which he had been expected to participate.

Early the next afternoon Billy drove to my office in a car bearing Michigan license plates. On one side of the car was this glaring statement: "Male High School denies admission to 17-year-old boy who had expressed his personal opinion against forced mixing of whites and Negroes." On the other side, this: "Witch hunters at Male High School barred a student because he had expressed personal opinion against forced race mixing."

The conference was brief, and I made no reference to the signs. I told Billy I was ruling him nonresident and, therefore, sustaining Mr. Milburn's position in not admitting him.

Within less than an hour Billy returned. He had learned from the Tuition Bureau that the nonresident fee for the remainder of the year would be $254.64. He said he would pay the tuition (as do 565 other nonresidents), and enroll at Male High the following Monday.

Because both Mr. Milburn and I were to be out of the city Monday through Thursday attending the annual meeting of the Southern Association of Colleges and Secondary Schools in Dallas, I called Billy on Sunday afternoon and read him the following statement before giving it to a reporter:

"We have no obligation for the education of a nonresident and are therefore free to deny admission.

"Billy has publicly stated his purpose to work against the established policies of our schools and confirmed this in a two-hour conference with Assistant City School Superintendent William F. Coslow and me.

"To accept him would be to set a precedent which would enable trouble-makers in any number from anywhere to enroll in our schools."

This action, supported fully by the Board of Education, did not appeal to all Louisvillians. There were some (and I am not referring to segregationists) who felt that we were on tenuous ground in refusing admission to a student because we considered him a

111

potential trouble-maker—that we should enroll him first and then expel him only if his conduct warranted it. I respect the feeling for justice inherent in such a position, but as long as Billy was clearly not a resident of Louisville I believed we were not only legally correct but wise to bar him when we did.

As for the segregationists, they did their best to make the Branham case a *cause célèbre*. They arranged a public meeting at which John Kasper, the Yankee segregationist who had made headlines in Tennessee, was the chief speaker (the others: Grubbs and Branham). And they threatened legal action to get young Branham into Male. Mr. Kasper, after paying his customary respects to the Supreme Court and federal implementation of its rulings, pledged his services to the Kentucky white Citizens Councils and its Louisville branch "as long as is necessary to stop this thing."

But only thirty-five persons attended the meeting.

On the Monday morning on which Billy presented himself again for admission to Male, ready to pay his tuition fee, he was again barred. He then went with three adult friends to confer with Mr. Coslow, but found this trip equally unrewarding.

A few days later we arranged a conference involving Branham's lawyers, Board of Education Attorney William T. Baskett, and myself. I reiterated that I was standing by the decision to bar Branham, and Branham's attorneys announced they were bringing suit to establish their client's rights.

During the Christmas holidays I received a Christmas card from Detroit. It was from Billy, wishing me "a happy, integrated New Year"—somewhat gentler in tone than his earlier declaration to me that, among other things, I was but "a misguided slave to the Jews who control the Louisville newspapers."

On December 31 I had a telephone call from a woman who did not identify herself. She said she had just moved to Louisville, lived at 1427 South Sixth Street, had a seventeen-year-old boy who was a senior in high school and a thirteen-year-old girl in seventh grade, and wished to know what schools they would attend. When I indicated that I recognized her, she somewhat hesitantly confirmed that she was Mrs. Alf Branham. I explained that her presence with the children in Louisville, while her husband was still in Detroit, did not necessarily establish residence—but that I would give her an answer on January 2 (after the New Year holiday).

On January 2, after a thorough discussion by administrative staff members and Male Principal Milburn, we decided that both children should be considered residents, conditioned on their father's joining them and their mother in Louisville as soon as he had settled his business affairs in Detroit. In the meantime, both were to be enrolled as resident students.

In a letter notifying Mrs. Branham of this decision, I made these points:

"Because Billy has made certain statements about his purpose to undertake to organize young people to oppose the program of desegregation in our schools, I think I should caution you, as his mother, that conduct of this nature which we think makes him a serious handicap to our schools can easily result in his suspension.

"Because Billy has been insistent to Mr. Coslow and me that the schools cannot be concerned with what he does in the community outside the school, I should tell you that we think we have this right and obligation and have exercised it when circumstances seemed to require it.

"If the children are to be in our schools, I hope that each of them will succeed well and prove a good school citizen."

On Monday, January 7, Billy enrolled at Male High School. There he soon made himself a bit of a nuisance in going frequently to the principal's office to complain that Negro pupils glared at him and mumbled something under their breath, that different white pupils showed an unfriendly spirit toward him, and that some of the teachers were circulating untrue reports about him.

A few days later Billy came to my office "to file a protest against a teacher at Male High." I instructed him to take up such matters with his principal.

On January 14 a reporter from the *Louisville Times*, acting on a tip that Billy was sponsoring a meeting near Male High, dropped by to investigate. He found Billy and several other students seated in booths, but Billy told him there was no "meeting." That, he said, would be at St. Helen's Commercial Club in suburban Shively on Wednesday night, January 16, at seven o'clock.

The reporter, James S. Pope, Jr., found Billy and thirteen other young people at the scheduled time and place. But Billy explained that he had decided the meeting should be private and asked Pope to leave. Pope did so, but stopped at a nearby drugstore where he could keep an eye on the club meeting. Another fifteen to twenty youngsters soon entered it.

The club has a beer license, and it was not long before Shively Police Chief Luther Melton dropped in to check on possible liquor-law violations by juveniles. Chief Melton, a large and not notably patient man who before that night had never heard of Branham, got a cold welcome.

Branham ordered him out.

Chief Melton did leave—but came back promptly with four policemen. To his explanation of his duties there, including the fact that state law forbids the meeting of minors in establishments licensed to sell alcoholic beverages, Branham retorted that he had rented the meeting place and cried: "Get out that door. You heard me, get out!"

"It took me off my feet very much for a young fellow to order me out," Chief Melton said in court later. He arrested Branham, took him to Children's Center (detention home for those under eighteen), and charged him with breach of the peace.

Chief Melton said he had seen no drinking in the club at the time of Branham's arrest. But he returned later, about nine o'clock, and arrested eleven other teen-agers—some for drinking, some for breach of peace. Two escaped while being booked but were caught later. Only three were school students—and only Branham was from Male. The others said they had met him in hangouts around Male and accepted his invitation to the party.

The club manager said the club had been reserved by Millard Grubbs.

Nine of the twelve youngsters arrested told the police that they had previously been sent to Children's Center or had been in Juvenile Court. The charges most frequently admitted were car theft and storehouse breaking.

Most of these cases, including Branham's, were still unfinished at the end of January. About him I said at the time of his arrest (he was released and came back to school next day) that, as is customary, we would await court developments before considering any possible action. (The charges against Branham later were dropped, and he remained in school.)

But I thought it worth while to tell the Billy Branham story at length for two reasons. It might explain in part why the leadership of those opposed to desegregation in Louisville has failed to arouse much support. And it is an unfinished story that could yet make more than local headlines.

On young Branham when he was arrested, police

found a letter offering him "bed and board indefinitely" if he could go to Knoxville to help organize the Knox County White Youth Council. It was dated January 11 and signed by John Kasper, executive secretary of the Seaboard White Citizens Councils of Washington, D. C., the New Jersey organizer and Columbia University graduate who in January was still free on bond pending appeal of a federal sentence for his role in the Clinton disorders.

"Integration in Knoxville was sought in Federal Court the other day by the niggers," the letter said.

"However, nigger-lover Frank Clement (the Governor of Tennessee) has been forced by the resistance at Clinton to go before the Legislature and seek a program which will maintain segregated schools in Tennessee.

"The day after the niggers sought admission to the Rule High School here [Knoxville], the kids dug five graves with wood headstones and seven-foot crosses. Two months work and we will have Tennessee organized statewide.

"I will go back to Kentucky with you and we can fight there to victory alongside Mr. Grubbs. If it can be done in Tennessee we can force the Kentucky Legislature to do the same there. Then Missouri, Arkansas, West Virginia, Maryland, Kansas, and D. C. to be regained. . ."

Billy Branham and Millard Grubbs were wasting no time in waiting for John Kasper's return. They spoke to a meeting of forty persons in Lawrenceburg, Kentucky, on January 19. Grubbs attacked the Supreme Court's segregation decisions as unconstitutional, sketched Branham's history and introduced him.

Young Branham said that he had been mistreated by Negroes in a Detroit school, and that this had led him to return to his native Kentucky to fight integration. He invited his hearers to sign applications for membership in the Citizens Council.

Two of the forty [the *Courier-Journal* reported] signed up.

How Much Integration?

The question has often been asked: Just how much desegregation did the Louisville schools achieve in 1956–57?

Complete, I would say, as far as principle is concerned: racial bars were dropped in every school. And that is all that the Court required, as more than one lower-court decision since 1955 has attested. But partial, of course, in terms of actual numbers. And none in teaching staffs.

In mid-October—after all of the post-registration transfer requests had been accommodated—a district-wide survey showed that of our seventy-five schools, fifty-five had mixed student bodies, eleven had all-white student bodies and nine all-Negro.

In the fifty-five schools with mixed student bodies

there were 73.6 per cent of all our 45,841 pupils: in the eleven all-white schools, 12.5 per cent, and in the nine all-Negro schools 13.9 per cent.

In the schools with mixed student bodies, the size of the minority group varied from one pupil to about 49 per cent. Two otherwise white schools each had a single Negro child and two otherwise Negro schools each had a single white pupil. One elementary school which the year before had white students only, this year had 55 per cent Negro and 45 per cent white. Another such school this year had a student body 45 per cent Negro and 55 per cent white. One junior high school with about 1,100 pupils had 30 per cent Negroes; another the same size had 20 per cent.

No white pupils enrolled in Central High School, which with 1,486 pupils accounted for 20.3 per cent of the total high-school enrollment. The five other senior high schools, all with mixed student bodies, had 5,832 pupils or 79.7 per cent. There were fifty to sixty Negroes in some, as few as two in one, situated in a virtually all-white residential district.

In the junior highs, mixed student bodies accounted for 73.8 per cent of the pupils, all-white schools for 17.8 per cent, and all-Negro schools for 8.4 per cent.

Another way of putting it: of the city's 12,010 Negro pupils, some 5,630 were in mixed schools, while 6,380 were in all-Negro schools; of the city's 33,831 white pupils, some 28,023 were in mixed schools, 5,808 in all-white schools.

In percentages: roughly 53 per cent of all Negro

pupils were in all-Negro schools, 47 per cent in integrated schools. Of white pupils, about 18 per cent were in all-white schools, 82 per cent in integrated schools.

We made no attempt to integrate faculties in the first year of transition. We had decided that we would tackle one major problem at a time—and desegregation of pupils had the first priority.

But on June 1, 1955—months before we adopted our detailed plan for school desegregation—I issued a public statement that no teachers, white or Negro, would lose their jobs because of integration. I added that eventually there would be teacher integration as well as pupil integration, because that would be the logical outcome of pupil integration.

In the spring of 1956 completion of the school assignment program showed the outline of pupil placement clearly enough for us to plan for the closing of five small erstwhile all-Negro schools and still to absorb their teachers in what had been all-Negro schools.

We kept our pledge to our teachers, white and Negro.

This first year of desegregation, nevertheless, is affording us valuable experience for the eventual integration of faculties. A great many Negroes are becoming accustomed to instruction from white teachers—although at least a few last-minute Negro transfer requests, I know, came from families apprehensive lest their children be treated unfairly by white teachers. Of greater importance, undoubtedly, is the fact that in the 1956–57 school year we have 87 white pupils attending six formerly all-Negro schools still staffed completely by Negro principals and teachers. There has been no serious friction in this field—although some white families, like the Negro families mentioned earlier, transferred their children to white-staffed schools during the first few days of the school year. And we count it an important contribution to our future program that a number of white parents this year have been high in their praise of the Negro teachers to whom they have entrusted their children's schooling.

There was another aspect in our first-year desegregation pattern of possible future importance—and certainly of more than passing interest to other communities: given their choice, a great many Negroes showed a preference for schools staffed by teachers of their own race. Apprehensions of a possibly chillier climate in mixed schools, I know, along with the articulate fear that white teachers might be unfair or that disorders in other Southern cities might spread to Louisville, accounted in part for this. It is also true that while some Negro community leaders urged a greater degree of pupil integration, others, including some Negro teachers and principals, sought to keep their pupils in their old schools.

The statistics cited above show that the greatest degree of integration occurred in the elementary schools, the least in the high schools—a fact explained in part, as I have mentioned, by the general excellence of Central High School, the loyalty of its students, and the fact that Central's location makes it convenient to larger numbers of Negro pupils. Most of the Negro pupils who enrolled in the city's other five senior high schools were not transfers from Central, but 1956 graduates of Negro junior highs.

What future patterns will be we have no means of knowing. Over the years I would expect that greater integration in the elementary schools of today would automatically lead to greater integration in the senior high schools, subject only to individual considerations of residential convenience. But the Louisville pattern this year suggests, as those in Indianapolis and other Northern cities have indicated before, that when given a genuine and unpressured choice many Negroes prefer to go to all-Negro schools or at least to those in which they will not be a small minority.

It may be worth adding that, despite some initial criticism of the permissive aspect of the Louisville program, its appeal to many Negro parents was quite as great as it was to others.

In schools with mixed student bodies, integration has been complete. The guiding rule is simply that a student is a student. In general, each school has continued its usual program of customary extracurricular activities.

An example in the social field is a school-sponsored dance in one of the senior high schools. The student council, after much discussion, decided to have the dance as heretofore, but open to Negro and white couples alike. Some fifteen or twenty Negro couples attended. Negroes danced with Negroes, and whites with whites—a custom still generally observed, I understand, at similar affairs of the University of Louisville.

Among the various units of the Parent-Teacher Association, many have a social hour with coffee or punch at the close of the meetings. In schools having both Negro and white patrons, in general, this program has continued without confusion or incident. But a few organizations have reported a slight decrease in attendance.

In athletics, competition of course has been open to all students. Though there were relatively few Negro pupils in erstwhile white senior high schools, several made the varsity football squads last fall, and two Negro players currently are seeing much action on the Male High basketball varsity. The junior high schools have no regular schedule of interschool competition but by arrangement between principals one junior high often plays another in basketball. Negro pupils are members of several junior high teams. And this year there has been a slight decrease in interschool competition. In one school for which this was true the principal explained that the space for spectators in the gym is so limited that he feared possible incidents arising as a result of Negro and white pupils jostling each other in the crowded situation inevitable with normal attendance.

Negro Ability: A Matter of Controversy

During this period some remarks of mine comparing Negro achievement with white attracted attention locally and nationally. The remarks were not new: I had discussed this subject as frankly, fairly and honestly as I could throughout our preparations for desegregation. But the national spotlight, sometimes beclouding the original context, made them susceptible to misinterpretation.

What I had to say about the competence of Negro teachers, in particular, led to an invitation for me to discuss the matter before a local Negro businessmen's group and a request from Louisville's Negro teachers to discuss it with them. I repeated at both meetings what I had said before. And I repeated, as I have done since on many a platform, what our comparative studies of Negro-white scholastic achievement showed —for example, that a ten-year analysis, based on records actually kept for twenty years, showed the average Negro sixth-grader in the Louisville schools to be nearly a year and a half behind the average white sixth-grader in scholastic achievement. And I explained to both local audiences, as I have to white and Negro school groups since, my earnest conviction that such facts must be faced and not be evaded or ignored.

Critics of my remarks, I think, made the mistake of assuming that by citing records of *achievement* I was accepting the racist view that the Negro is inherently unequal to the white man in *ability*. And there were some who said that, due to my long experience in Southern schools, I was simply reflecting "Southern bias."

What had particularly irritated our Louisville Negro teachers was a magazine statement of mine that "the average white teacher is considerably superior to the average Negro teacher in competence as a person to teach children," and, following my explanation that this stemmed from social, economic, environmental and cultural factors, this rhetorical question:

"How can a person come out of a slummy, crime-ridden area of the city, with poor churches and few of the things that go to enrich life—how can a person come out of such a background the equal of one who comes out of a more cultured home in a more cultured community, etc.?"

At the Louisville meeting of nearly 400 Negro teachers I expressed keen regret that more background information did not accompany my original statements. And I reiterated a point of old and continuing belief:

"There are good teachers and poor teachers of both races. There are excellent teachers in both races but on the average the Negro teacher is less good than the white teacher."

To the Louisville Negro teachers I distributed some 400 copies of "Problems of Evaluating Test Scores of White and Negro Teachers" by Arthur L. Benson, director of teacher examinations for Educational Testing Service, Princeton, N. J. This detailed 1954 study of several tests, given to Negro and white students and teachers in a number of states, showed the Negro average significantly below the white average score in every instance.

I would be the last to argue that tests alone are a good measure of competence. I do contend that they are one objective factor in measuring competence.

But nothing of this sort, and certainly no revelations of scholastic deficiencies among Negro students, it seems to me, ought to surprise anyone. Leaders of the Negro race long since have established Negro ability to achieve greatness. But in a land where a majority of all Negroes for scores of years, at the hands of the law or by custom, or both, have suffered educational, economic, and general environmental discrimination, I do not see how anyone could expect the average Negro student or the average Negro teacher to match the *achievement* standards of those not so handicapped. Indeed, it seems to me, this was the foundation of the Supreme Court's decision that racial segregation in the schools is inherently a denial of equality of opportunity.

The Louisville meeting of Negro teachers was moderated by Lyman T. Johnson, social sciences teacher at Central High (whose suit in 1949 had resulted in the opening of the University of Kentucky to Negro students). Mr. Johnson later told a reporter that, while my earlier and incomplete statement had been taken as an insult, "now we are convinced that he did not intend it as an insult." And the teachers applauded my closing statement:

"I have a lot to learn about this question of race relations. I may make mistakes, but they will be as fair as my heart dictates. I don't want anything unfortunate to happen to cause our progress to fail in the days and weeks and months that lie ahead."

As easy as it is for a discussion of this question to cause misunderstanding or resentment, I have found a great many Negro teachers and school officials in Louisville and throughout the country in agreement with its basic premise and with the necessity for the public schools to face the problem honestly. In recent months I have received hundreds of letters and telegrams from persons all over the United States and from several foreign countries (about 10 per cent of them, I might add, have been critical or rudely abusive, the other 90 per cent complimentary or approving). A fair percentage came from Negroes, in and out of Louisville. Many of them have given me cause for gratification, and perhaps I should cite one of the most recent. It came on January 17, 1957, from Emory A. James, principal of Indianapolis' John Hope School:

"I deemed it a great pleasure to have had the honor to be associated with you on the recent Sunday Forum in which you so ably, fairly and frankly discussed the desegregation program.

"Your humane and Christian approach to this program in Louisville is to be most highly commended.

Your straightforward enunciation of facts won for you many friends among my people. In the audience (a majority of which was Negro) I noted some who have always been skeptical of the sincerity of white administrators, nodding their approval of your utterances as you spoke and answered questions.

"I am firm in the belief that the Negro as one of the minority groups must get the best possible education obtainable and in the process evaluate every inter-racial action on its individual merit rather than upon a basis of something done against the Negro.

"As educated Negroes we must enable ourselves to sit down with whites and impassionately and un-biasedly discuss our problems, facing them as they are, and together with our white brethren seek a common-sense solution which shall do credit to both races.

"May I again commend you for your courage, understanding, tenacity and forthrightness in the cause of true justice.

"To many you are a real man endeavoring to do what the Master would have all of us do—'ministrare non ministrari.' May God give you many more years to propagate your common-sense theories."

On another controversial matter I welcome the opportunity to repeat my televised opinion of last fall that both of our major political parties failed in their obligations to the public by not giving a clean-cut endorsement, without any reservations, of the Supreme

Court's desegregation decision. It would have helped immeasurably everywhere if on this, the greatest human problem of our generation, they had adopted a common platform and taken the desegregation issue out of the campaign.

How Much Success?: An Interim Evaluation

One half of a school year, clearly, is not enough on which to base any final judgments of success or failure in a new program. But at the end of the first semester it is possible to report that the program has worked far more smoothly than we had dared hope, that there have been no serious incidents, and that our teachers and pupils are learning a great deal about the adjustment necessary in working successfully with people of another race. Many of our teachers have had to work harder, as we all expected, and the first-semester experience confirms our earlier belief that real effort will be required to maintain current standards in many of the desegregated schools.

These general conclusions vary a bit from school to school, of course. Some light on them may be gleaned from sample reports from our interviews with several principals late in January. At Male High (about fifty Negro pupils in an enrollment of nearly 1,200), Principal William S. Milburn, who has held that position

129

since 1931, reported that his Negro students "must have been hand-picked." Their school records showed remarkably high I.Q.s to begin with, their scholastic achievement has not only been equal with that of white students but their group percentage of high grades has exceeded that of white students, and their attendance record has been better. Matters have gone well.

"We have come a long way since 1932," said the ruddy-faced and energetic Mr. Milburn, who among other distinctions was the first principal to be elected president of the Southern Association of Colleges and Secondary Schools (1955) and who is now serving his third year as president of the Louisville Board of Aldermen. "In that year Male High's track team had a meet with Indiana's Corydon High School—and the Indiana team had one Negro on it. I all but lost my job over that."

Mr. Milburn observed that there has been a tremendous increase in minor disciplinary problems at Male ever since 1951—tardiness, absenteeism, unruliness, disobedience, rule-breaking, thieving, and impertinence to teachers. But desegregation, he said, had had no effect on this deplorable pattern. Except, as noted, that the Negro attendance record is better than the white.

Manual High Principal A. J. Ries said, "I don't know whether we are on a honeymoon or not, but so far everything has gone remarkably well."

Manual has only 18 Negro pupils in the senior high

school, nearly 100 in junior high (total enrollment: 2,450). As at Male, the senior high-school students are doing well. But in the junior high a majority of the Negro pupils rate in the lower third of their class scholastically, and their percentage of absenteeism is higher.

But all groups have adjusted well, Mr. Ries said, and there have been no serious interracial incidents. The most serious involved a non-school white youth who pulled a switchblade knife on white pupils during a football rally. But he was promptly disarmed by his companions and turned over to police.

"The closest we came to real trouble was about three months ago," said Mr. Ries, "when a Negro pupil ended a campus altercation with the declaration that he was going home and returning with a gun. He didn't, thanks to the timely persuasion of the Crime Prevention Bureau with the pupil and his parents, and nothing more happened. That particular pupil later dropped out of school, but his scholastic record alone, I think, accounted for that."

And here are brief representative excerpts from reports by principals of other schools:

Belknap School (368 white pupils, one Negro): ". . . The Negro child has been accepted on the playground, in the lunchroom, and is chosen for a partner like all the others."

Perry School (611 Negroes, one white pupil): ". . . Our one white second-grader and his classmates have worked and played together very well.

His mother has visited the classroom several times. She always brings her two smaller children with her and they chat with the other children and share the classroom activities. Our boys and girls are learning the essential things that will help them develop into American citizens."

Manly Junior High School (752 white pupils, 292 Negroes): ". . . The school has run rather smoothly. There have been, and are, problems. By far the largest number of Negro children are trying to do the right thing. . . . Recently there have been more disciplinary problems, proportionately more with Negro pupils. This has been intraracial for the most part rather than interracial. In general, problems this year have not been very different from those of the past. . . . Part of our difficulties stems from the fact that the colored pupils are not as advanced academically as the white children: certainly there are exceptions, but results of class work and tests substantiate this. . . . On the whole, we have found the Negro children to be quite polite. When it has been necessary to call in their parents, they have responded quite readily. . . . The faculty here feels that our situation has not been an easy one. We were determined at the outset to make the plan work. Constant vigilance has led some to express themselves as being quite tired at the end of the day.

"On the whole, desegregation has worked better than we feared it might."

F. T. Salisbury School (220 white pupils, 216 Negroes): ". . . Our teachers have taken hold of every situation in the truly American way. Concern for the individual child has been uppermost in mind. As a child faced a personal problem the teachers learned and advised. If a social problem seemed to cause unhappiness, individual guidance, enlistment of the group's help, suggestions of need for better co-operation on the part of the parents, and finally arrangement within the faculty to place the child within the classroom situation wherein he can develop his greatest potentialities, has been our course of action.

". . . Teachers of the first and second grades have expressed the opinion that it has taken a longer time to establish the routine habits within their classrooms: There is an impulsiveness that requires strict restraint. Patience is the essential characteristic we are trying to stress within our own personalities.

". . . We have had a satisfactory relationship among our parents. . . . The team of mothers who took part in the Mothers' March on Polio was made up of mothers of both races."

California School (165 Negro pupils, 137 white): ". . . Teachers and parents found that the children (who had been living and playing in a Negro-white neighborhood) immediately accepted the new situation, on the surface, at least. . . . A few parents asked for seat changes. Some came, saw the large number of Negroes, and decided to ask for transfers. Seat changes were not granted. Transfers were determined at the Board of Education.

". . . As time went on, children accepted each other more and more as individuals. What may have been surface acceptance in many cases now seems to be a deeper feeling of acceptance. Teachers can tell it by the way children treat each other: little things that they say about each other and to each other in school situations.

". . . In the P.T.A., parents have worked together on several projects to raise money. . . . All in all the change-over has progressed smoothly. Very few incidents of strong feelings have come about. Most of the parents who would have been potential disturbances were satisfied by having been given choices of schools in the spring.

". . . Many fine things have been developing through the processes of integration. A better understanding between Negro and white children seems to be slowly establishing itself. Teachers are recognizing many potentialities in the Negro children. Parents are more slowly accepting each other, but progress is evident. The neighborhood seems to feel a little more relaxed about the situation.

"The California School faculty has expressed itself many times on the fact that the transition has been so smooth. This did *not just happen*. Co-operation, sympathy and understanding on the part of teachers, parents, pupils and community, under excellent leadership, brought this about."

Foster School (600 white pupils, 89 Negroes): ". . . Evidence of polite acceptance. . . . Occasional complaints from white parents and Negro parents—

the calm polite responses of the teachers made the parents feel better.

". . . We know that unhealthy tensions still exist. Deep-seated, long-standing forces of opinion and sentiment are obviously involved. Segregation practices cannot be wished away or eradicated by an order. Time, calm teachers, and polite, understanding parents will change public opinion. The credit for the ease with which our school has carried out the program of instruction this year is due entirely to the attitude of the teachers and parents. Everyone has tried to build respect for the worth of the individual."

Frederick Douglass School (215 Negro pupils, 42 white): "Our boundary lines cover an extended area of the two races. From the very beginning the plan of integration has worked . . . all our classes are integrated . . . there have been few adjustments to be made.

"The parents of our new children (white) have accepted our teachers very readily and have expressed themselves freely on the subject of integration and how well satisfied they are with the educational progress their children have made this year. Some have sent notes expressing appreciation for the courtesies shown and the interest taken in their children. When two white parents were forced to move from our district, they came to express their regret. Parental co-operation has been splendid . . . the children are seemingly happy and on numerous occasions have expressed a liking for their teachers, their classmates, and the school in general.

"We have had discipline problems, problems of retardation, and others, as heretofore. But ours have not been problems of desegregation. . . . In this light we are especially proud of the school's Christmas activities. The Sixth Grade's mixed boys' chorus sang at many institutions, and was seen on TV when they sang at the Children's Center and the Louisville General Hospital; many parents called the school to express pleasure at seeing their children on TV . . . more of this happened when Mrs. Aora Lilly's first-grade class was honored to appear on the 'Home Show' (NBC) with Mr. Carmichael . . . the two classes in Special Education (Ungraded and Crippled Children) presented a play at Christmas time, with their parents and school officials as special guests. It was most gratifying to see how well pleased the parents were.

"Our success . . . is due largely to the efforts of the teachers, who are teachers dedicated to the job and are truly interested in children. No matter how poor the economic background of the child, they have tried to make him realize that he is important, that he possesses dignity and worth and is due the respect of everyone, and that the same is expected of him."

A Note on Discipline

Beyond an expected increase at some schools in the occasional use of vulgar or obscene language, a few pushing and shoving incidents, and such burdensome but nonracial minor lapses as described by Male Principal Milburn, our disciplinary record for the first half of the 1956–57 school year was a pleasant surprise to a good many Louisvillians.

There were, as I have said, no major incidents. Aside from the close co-operation of school and police authorities and parents, this was accounted for, in important degree, by the kind of press coverage accorded minor incidents—any one of which, given sensational or exaggerated attention by a hostile press or radio and television newscasts, might have fanned racial tensions to the danger point. But, though the gentlemen of the press gave thorough and efficient coverage to what was happening, there was no sensation-mongering either in the press or on the airlanes —and the editorial columns as well as the local commentators gave vigorous support to the cause of peaceful transition.

There was one initially alarming incident, for instance, during September registration. The first report: a teen-age white girl had been "roughed up" by several Negro students, and a twelve-year-old white boy had drawn a knife to defend her. But students kept their heads, police quickly arrived—and news accounts gave calm play to the actual story as determined by the police investigation: the white girl didn't belong at the school in question, twice had been suspended from her own school for "belligerence," precipitated an oral "fight" with Negroes on the sidewalk, had not been attacked, and was held wholly responsible. Her valiant young would-be defender got some wise counseling, and the girl's case disappeared in the accustomed quiet of Juvenile Court ministrations.

This enlightening incident may explain why Police Chief Heustis, the enthusiastic careerist who rose from patrolman in 1933 to Chief in 1946 (and who has been kept in his appointive office by a long line of what he calls "independent-minded mayors"), was among the few Louisvillians *not* surprised by the lack of serious incidents.

"I like to think," he said early in February, "that a big factor in all this is the reputation of the Police Department for fairness and efficiency. People in both races know that the police are going to do their best to be absolutely fair, whether the police are white or Negro, and no matter what the race or economic status of those involved in any kind of incident.

"That reputation was being built a long time ago, before my time, and it was helped a lot by Dave McCandless when he was Safety Director, so I am not exactly breaking my arm to pat myself on the back. I remember the big kick I got back in 1935, when I was a corporal in the Accident Prevention Section, and heard two Negroes talk about an accident we had rushed to in a Negro residential area.

"A white man had 'shot' a red light and crashed into a Negro's car—nobody hurt to speak of, but quite a bit of damage to both cars. There was a crowd around, of course, and I heard one Negro say to another: 'Bet you a million they won't do a thing to that driver—he's a white man.' The other said: 'Ain't got a million, but I lay you ten to one they do—you just don't know nothin' about our police.'

"I hope the second Negro collected, because he won. Our investigation showed the white man at fault, and on our recommendation the Negro owner of the damaged car signed a warrant against the white driver.

"I don't mean to say that we have achieved perfection in our department, not by a long shot. But I will say it's been eight or nine years since anyone's come into my office to use foul language about our Negro officers, like one white man did after his wife was handed a ticket for parking her Cadillac directly in front of a theater while he walked down the street to buy some tickets at the Armory for some show or other.

"He wanted the Negro officer fired, of course, because 'no black so-and-so is going to talk to my wife, much less hand her a ticket,' etc. I told him to get out of my office within two minutes or I might—anyway, he got. I knew the officer in question, I knew he was carrying out specific orders in that traffic-congested area around the Armory, and I didn't even bother to ask him or anybody else about it until a couple of days later. He had been, as I expected, a model of politeness and efficiency in a situation obviously distasteful to him.

"And we no longer have people calling us up to enforce segregation 'laws' that aren't on the books any more and in most cases never were. And anybody calling us up knows they'd better be in the clear themselves before they try to pin charges against others.

"One of the big things that has helped us build this mighty useful reputation for fairness is the keen loyalty and the good work of our Negro members."

Colonel Heustis paused for reflection.

"I don't mean to say that everybody likes it," he said. "Of course some don't. Your grandfather and mine probably would be shocked to the gills—and there are still some grandfathers around.

"But that's what I said about the school situation pretty much from the beginning—it wasn't the kids or the younger folks we might have to worry about, but the 'grandfathers.' And fortunately they have been content to get things off their chest with nothing much worse than talk."

A Veteran Teacher's Views

And what about Miss Freda Zuercher, the silver-haired Manual High teacher who had been so enthusiastic about the way things worked on the opening day of school?

Still enthusiastic, she said at the end of the

first semester, about the "marvelous way" in which pupils of both races "get along together." But better acquainted with what comparative school-achievement records had led her to expect: most of her twenty-five Negro junior high pupils (down five from September) are not "up" scholastically, the majority being in the "lower third." And she just doesn't know what to do about one tall, well-built, well-mannered Negro in a ninth-grade English class. Nothing wrong with him at all—except that, like an occasional white pupil she's had, he simply can't read. Or learn. Double pity, too, because he would make a fine addition to the football squad.

But though not one of Miss Zuercher's Negro pupils has attained a scholastic rating of "Excellent," there are several rated "Very Good." And there are several in both groups of whom she said, "I have become very fond of them—and I believe they like me, too."

But the behavior of all is about par for that of white pupils, though one Negro girl is inclined to "argue a bit too much with pupils of both races." And the percentage of industrious workers is good.

Some other white teachers of her acquaintance, Miss Zuercher said, have been less fortunate in having a higher percentage of very poor Negro pupils, with a consequent increase of their work-load. Hers has increased, too, "but not too much." Speech is the big stumbling block of many of her "lower thirds"— enunciation, spelling, limited vocabularies, "a total lack of acquaintance with the language as most people speak it." Some of her white pupils have this problem too, especially those coming from really poor homes; and others who know better are just plain careless or lazy—"but not as many."

"One trouble in both races," Miss Zuercher said cheerfully, "is that we have a heavy load of pupils who ought not be in school anywhere, or certainly not in regular classes. But it is a public-school responsibility, and we have to do the best we can. And after forty years in the Louisville schools, I still like teaching. . . .

"Some of my Negro pupils have shown marked improvement in recent months. I think mixed schooling will help them all, except in the truly hopeless cases —and we have some white pupils in that category, too. I think it is a good thing not only for them but for the community. I guess I get some of my ideas about this from my church—I belong to the Church of Christ, you know. But I think nearly all our teachers feel pretty much this way by now, too—the few who wouldn't 'got out' long ago when we first began having mixed teachers' committees."

For whatever degree of success we have had (and to us it has been most gratifying), I would list these as the most important factors in it:

(1) A long period of good racial relations and interracial adjustment in other fields, on a gradual basis, before we attempted to desegregate the schools.

(2) Prompt and clear-cut acceptance of the decision of the Supreme Court as the law.

(3) Prompt and clear-cut announcement, following the Court's "how and when" ruling, that it would be carried out without undue delay or any effort at subterfuge.

(4) Careful, systematic and thorough preparation of pupils and teachers and the community at large for the change.

(5) Full co-operation of City and County officials, and a County program similar to ours in timing and objectives.

(6) A friendly press, alert and thorough in its news coverage and vigorous in its editorial comments.

Beyond all this, of course, was the firm foundation on which all else was built: the respect of Louisville's citizens for law and order, and their recognition of the human rights involved. And among these citizens, for the leadership and the untiring efforts they contributed to the program, I shall always hold in special esteem the Louisville Board of Education, the administrative and supervisory staff, the principals and teachers and all other employees of the schools, the 46,000 pupils, and the 33,000 members of the Parent-Teacher Associations.

Outside the Classroom

Outside the schools there were several developments from September 1956, to February 1957 of considerable community interest.

An October survey showed that of 221 school districts in Kentucky 40 had no Negro children and 92 had begun a program of desegregation. Others were making plans—or just "waiting."

Kentucky's Methodists in November held a two-day Interracial Leadership Conference in Louisville, first of its kind in the South. To the 200 conferees Mayor Broaddus reported that Louisville had ended segregation "in all areas under jurisdiction of local government." This, the Mayor said, was "a development of years, mirroring the community conscience." The conference workshop recommended integration of the Negro branch of the Methodist Church into the Methodist white jurisdiction. A Negro Methodist Bishop, J. W. E. Bowen of Atlanta, predicted that his people would not rush to join white churches but would prefer their own Negro ministers. What they want under an integrated church, he said, is simply the freedom to join white churches if they desire.

It was to this interracial conference that Dr. Robert I. Kutak, the University of Louisville sociologist, submitted his detailed study of Louisville's Negro community (referred to in Chapter II). Dr. Kutak, noting that economic factors had forced the closing of public school kindergartens, recommended that the churches desegregate their kindergartens. A subsequent newspaper survey disclosed that several white Protestant churches already had done so, some in fact, some in policy, while three churches primarily Negro in membership had enrolled white pupils in the past and still maintained an "open" policy. (Only a few of the city's Catholic churches have kindergartens.)

And around the city, the delegates could observe, there were some eating places and some hotels now open to all. Elsewhere, if they looked, they could see more Negroes than in past years among the congregations of some of the city's churches.

In the National election of November 6, Kentuckians gave President Eisenhower a majority of 95,740 in a total vote of 1,053,804. In Louisville, an analysis by Dr. Louis C. Kesselman of the University of Louisville showed that five per cent fewer Negroes voted than in 1952. But Negroes voted just about as everybody else in the city did—56.7 per cent for Ike, compared with a city-wide total of 56.1 for Ike. From the registration figures and the voting record, Dr. Kesselman found "more of a decline of Negro support for the Democratic party in Louisville than a switch to the Republicans."

In the same election, the States Rights Party, with Millard Grubbs of the white Citizens Councils a candidate for the United States Senate, got a total of 2,657 votes in the state. In Louisville and Jefferson County the party total was 357.

Of thirteen nurses' training schools in Kentucky, ten now accept Negro students, the Kentucky Council on Human Relations reported in December. The same organization reported later that 112 Negro teachers were then teaching in Kentucky schools having white students. Most were in Louisville.

And in January 1957, seven Negro schools prepared to compete for the first time with white schools in basketball tournament competition. (Interracial athletic competition in Kentucky was not new, but this was.) Among the eleven Negro schools accepted as members of the Kentucky High School Athletic Association, the seven qualified for tournament competition by playing a minimum of twelve games against six member schools. Top-rated to win the state championship in the spring: Louisville Central, winner the two preceding years of the National Negro High School championship.

For 1956, Station WHAS-TV did not make its usual "Man of the Year" award. Instead it named three "Personalities of the Year" in Louisville, all for their roles in successfully desegregating the schools. I was deeply gratified to be named one of them. The others were Jefferson County Superintendent Van Hoose and Monsignor Pitt of the Catholic School Board.

In presenting engraved silver platters to us (during a telecast), Barry Bingham, president of the station and of the *Courier-Journal* and the *Louisville Times*, said:

"The fears and tensions of generations do not pass overnight. But here is a community that has struck out with courage on a hard road. Louisville people have learned in an unusual degree how to make a workable pattern of life out of opposing points of view. They have learned, in a word, tolerance."

What the Public Thinks

Last fall I expressed publicly the opinion that had Louisvillians been polled beforehand, a majority would have voiced opposition in varying degrees to school desegregation. This was our belief, from a close acquaintance with the community, in the period preceding 1955—and was largely responsible, of course, for the community-wide preparations we made.

During that two-year program there was obviously not much to be gained from any new poll of public opinion. Our course of compliance was set, and there was no polling. But we decided last fall that it might be worth while to sample public attitudes after the first half-year of the desegregated program. For this we engaged the industrial-consultant firm of Kemper & Associates, headed by Dr. Raymond A. Kemper, the University of Louisville psychologist. The firm has made many market-research and public-opinion studies for a large number of clients, and it was Dr. Kemper's pollsters who produced the 1949 findings cited earlier on how Louisvillians felt about park and high-school desegregation.

The poll was made in January of this year. Tables detailing its findings may be of special interest to some readers, and therefore are included in the Appendix.

Here it is sufficient to report the major findings of

the survey. The one surprise it yielded, to citizens and school leaders closest to the desegregation program, was that only 24 per cent disapprove completely, and propose an attempt to change back to the old policy. We thought that figure would be higher.

We had asked Dr. Kemper to check (1) attitudes toward the policy of school desegregation initiated last September, (2) opinions on the way the school policy change was brought about, and (3) opinions about some other aspects of desegregation in Louisville.

(In 1949 some 71.9 per cent of the Louisvillians polled had opposed park desegregation. In 1957 some 54 per cent, following actual desegregation last summer, still didn't approve the idea—and 65 per cent, including 9 per cent of the Negroes polled, said "no" to this question: "Do you think that all city swimming pools should be open to Negroes?")

From the standpoint of the schools, these were the major findings of the Kemper poll:

(1) On the question of school desegregation, there were wide degrees of opinion—but 69 per cent accepted the change while 7 per cent didn't care much one way or the other, and only 24 per cent registered complete disapproval and proposed an attempt to turn the clock back.

The majority breakdown showed that 16 per cent fully approved, 30 per cent accepted the change as something that is "right," "inevitable," or "sensible," and 23 per cent accepted the policy as an accomplished fact although they disapproved of it on principle.

(2) A majority, including many who disapproved of the change itself, felt that the procedure was acceptable and well planned.

(3) Although a majority of Negroes approved, about 12 per cent disapproved the change in some degree.

(4) There seemed to be little difference between the responses of white Protestants and white Catholics.

(5) There appeared to be no significant difference of opinion between men and women or between age groups.

(6) People with some college education seemed more likely to approve the desegregation policy than did those with less formal education.

(7) Respondents in the upper-middle socio-economic group showed more approval than did members of other socio-economic groups in the white segment of the population.

(8) The opinion of parents with a child or children enrolled in integrated schools did not differ significantly from that of other parents.

△

Something about Myself:
A Personal Word

A GREAT MANY PEOPLE in recent months have asked
me about my background, my early education,
my own philosophy on the whole segregation-deseg-
regation question. Some of all that, surely, is implicit
in the record. I count it a pleasure to make that
record more explicit by telling here something of the
influences and the happenings that helped make me
today, I like to think, not unlike many other Southerners of my background and my generation—born
poor, but determined to rise above it, passionately

hungry for learning, and deeply influenced by the teachings of Christ.

I was born and raised on a farm in the pine-and-cotton country of Clay County, Alabama, sixty-four years ago. I was the oldest of eight children, all the others girls. My mother had less than a high-school education. My father had what would today be a junior college education. He taught country schools and farmed, until his marriage at thirty-six, and then he devoted his time to the farm and the family.

We children all worked at the jobs that are to be done in a farm home. One of the many good things about such a life was that there were so many things that very small children could do. Wise parents knew how to match the child and the job. There was kindling wood to bring in, floors to sweep, beds to make, leaves to rake, vegetables to gather, hickory nuts and walnuts to pick up, strawberries, dewberries, black-berries, huckleberries and wild plums, apples and peaches to pick, flowers to weed, dishes to wash, tables to set, fires to keep, cats, dogs, pigs, sheep and lambs to feed. And, in season, as we grew, there was cotton to hoe and to pick.

I moved gradually from the small-child chores to the adult tasks and was plowing full-time the spring I was nine—and outraged when given the oldest, slowest horse.

Our home was rather strict Presbyterian. Nothing was done on Sunday that could be done on Saturday. Saturday afternoon the wood and kindling boxes were filled and extra wood put on the porch, the amount related to the mildness or severity of the weather, with generous allowance for poor forecasting. A good part of the Sunday food was cooked on Saturday. No churning on Sunday. Extra corn was shucked for feeding the hogs and the horses.

From the time we were four or five weeks old we were taken to Sunday School each Sunday morning and, after Sunday School on the fourth Sunday in each month and one fifth Sunday during the year, to church—our preacher serving three other churches by the same pattern. Ours was the only Presbyterian church in the county. For two weeks each summer there was camp meeting at our church. For comfort the services were held in an "arbor" which was a well-built frame affair, with a rather high gable roof joined directly to the church but longer and wider than the church. Ten or a dozen of the members had built "tents" to which they moved for the camp meeting period—normally two weeks, with services morning and night. If the preaching was unusually good and interest high the meetings lasted longer. The afternoons afforded opportunity for many social and recreational activities for the children and young people. Sometimes the older youngsters had responsibilities at home that denied them these social activities, but they were resourceful in making exchanges and partnerships to get the work done.

Sunday in our home was a day of rest and relaxation from the strenuous work of the week. No reading

of newspapers or other secular materials, no singing
except hymns, no organized games, no noisy activities.
There were long walks in the fields and woods and
gathering nuts, berries, and fruits. There were visits to
and from neighbors. There was a reasonable time
given to study of the Bible and Sunday School lesson,
with some memorizing, and to reading the few religious books we had and the thirty-two volumes in
the Sunday School library. In spite of the restrictions,
Sunday was a happy day. Through college days I
continued to observe Sunday in very much the pattern
of my childhood and still try to reserve it primarily
for Sunday School and church and family.

My father was a strong believer in education. We
children attended the one-room school a mile and a
half away when it was in session—usually four or
five months in winter and six or eight weeks in
summer. He was a trustee and employed the teacher.
There was not enough tax money to pay the teacher
for even this short term. Father would contribute
all he could afford and raise what he could from
other patrons, but would never consent to a tuition
charge, because of the children whose parents couldn't
pay.

During the spring I was sixteen, I reached the decision that I would enter college in the fall. The year
was 1909. I got catalogues of three or four colleges,
and decided on the University of Alabama. Because
I had no education but that gained in the one-room
school, I borrowed money from Father (he refused

repayment) to order the books I should study to prepare for entrance examinations.

My father said he would give me $125 to start my
freshman year and co-sign notes for money I would
have to borrow. He would also give me free use of
land to make a crop each summer. All he asked was
that I should see that my sisters got a college education later.

At that time the University of Alabama would accept a student with thirteen units of credit and permit the other two units to be earned in "Sub-Freshman" courses in the University. I planned that these
should be English and Latin. With complete ignorance
of the enormity of what I was attempting, I began to
study algebra, geometry, physics, grammar, ancient
history, medieval and modern history, English, civics,
agriculture and Latin. My time for study was in the
evenings after a full day of work on the farm, on rainy
days, at school (which was eight weeks that summer),
and about three weeks after the summer school closed.
I remember that I studied till midnight on Saturday
night before I was to leave Monday for the University.

Mathematics was easy for me, so I got along well
with algebra, and fairly well, thanks to some help
from Father and from the teacher in the summer
school, with geometry. I read through two physics
books. Because I enjoyed history I covered all the
books, though not too thoroughly. I made very broad
outlines for ease in reviewing. Because Father thought

grammar very important, I sought to master it—which was to serve me well in Latin and Greek, as well as English, in college. There just wasn't enough time for mastery of plane geometry and I covered only about thirty lessons in first-year Latin.

With no conception of how unprepared I was, I went to the University expecting to take entrance examinations. When I went to the Dean's office to arrange for the examination, he asked the name of my (high) school. I gave "Midway." To this he replied that they had had several students from Midway and they had done well. This I knew was a mistake but I saw no reason to challenge the statement. He then inquired what courses I had had and I named the subjects I had studied. When he asked the text used in one course, I gave the texts for all of them and the authors. I knew I wanted to register for the A.B. degree, which meant Latin and Greek. I explained that I had not had Caesar and Cicero, nor the literature course with my grammar, and would therefore expect to take "Sub-Freshman" Latin and English.

To my utter surprise, the Dean made out a schedule of classes for me and told me when to report. Since I had come two or three days early to take the entrance exams, I had some time on my hands. I went at once to the bookstore and bought the cheapest second-hand books I could and went immediately to work on the first part of each. This enabled me to go to classes the first day with work prepared several days ahead—algebra, solid geometry, American history and Greek. I had read the English but had little background for it, except the grammar. I could do nothing with Caesar, because I had had almost no first-year Latin.

I had Latin and Greek with the same professor. While Greek was hard for me, I was getting along all right. The professor soon discovered that I knew no Latin and patiently laid out a program of study of first-year Latin for me, on which I worked every hour I could spare and reported to him from time to time. He told me to watch carefully in class and he would always call on me for something that had already been covered that day. Never did a bewildered freshman have a kinder and more understanding teacher. Never was there a more grateful freshman. In two months I had mastered first-year Latin and asked that I have no more special consideration in class.

Though my general preparation for college was wholly inadequate, by hard work and close attention in class, I was holding on successfully in all other courses.

If I was poorly prepared scholastically, I was even less well prepared in all other ways except desire for an education, willingness to work and the ability to work far into the night, five nights in the week. There was never study on Sunday—not even after midnight Saturday. Sunday School and church Sunday mornings; resting, visiting, and long walks in the afternoon.

Until I went to college, I had been more than

twenty miles from home only twice. Each of these trips was to visit relatives, one a forty-mile trip and the other fifty—by horse-and-buggy, of course. The trip to the University was my first train ride and on the wait-over to change trains in Birmingham, I saw my first streetcar. It was two months later that I was to see my first "moving picture show."

In Southern colleges of that day hazing was almost universal and often very severe. There was much criticism of it in the newspapers. To avoid it, I decided I would live in a private home—but I would also go prepared. On the farm I always carried a heavy, long-bladed pocketknife. On Saturday afternoon, in preparation for the next week at the University, I put a very keen edge on all its blades. Father noticed it and asked why. I said I didn't propose to be hazed and might need it.

Father was a mild, quiet man—but not lacking in courage. He said he had never been to college and didn't know how to advise me, except that he hoped I wouldn't let anybody "run over" me, but that in protecting myself I must be careful not to kill anybody. He then pointed out that I was a bit impetuous and rather young to be going off on my own; but that I knew what was right and what was wrong and that he was willing to trust me. "But," he said—and I can hear him now—"but don't act hastily."

Those words spoken nearly forty-eight years ago have served me well countless times. The first week I was at the University, when threatened with hazing,

I was prepared to use the knife and so stated—but the hazer didn't press the question. In a brief time I had become a little acquainted with college life and put the knife away. I don't like to think what would have happened if I had been pressed those first few days!

College was a wonderful experience for me. I stuck too close to books, especially my first two years, and missed too much of the other values that college had. There was much I did get. During the four years I never missed Sunday School or church. The University class at the Presbyterian church was taught by a woman. She knew how to make the lessons tie into life. The minister was not outstanding; the music was good to excellent; the congregation friendly and the whole service satisfying.

The Philomathic Literary Society gave me in freshman year some of the values which I would have got in "elocution"—required of freshmen but for me delayed until sophomore year because of conflict with my "Sub-Freshman" English. After "elocution" in sophomore year I took Public Speaking in junior year and Argumentation in senior year. These courses I have valued greatly, partly because of my admiration for the man who taught them. He took a personal interest in all his students and gave most generously of his time to counsel and advise with those who would come to him.

He also taught me Sophomore English. He required weekly themes, carefully corrected every one, and had a conference with every student twice a month on his themes. A man of strong convictions, he often spent time challenging, commending or condemning (constructively) the content of themes. I shall never forget one such conference I had with him. I had never been able to get better than *B*-plus on a theme. On this occasion one of my themes had in bold red on the back of it, "*A*—almost *A*-plus on Theme, *F*-(?) on Character."

With tremendous earnestness he said in substance: Carmichael, you've never given me an *A* theme before. Now, you have perfectly vile, immoral content and it merits an *A* grade. Does that mean that you are at your best only when you are dealing with immoral material? And so forth.

I had described, I suppose with approval, an altercation between a white boy and a Negro boy in which the white boy came out on top when the Negro boy had been right.

On other occasions when content pleased him, this good teacher was as generous in praise as he was severe in criticism in this case. To him I owe much. He hated sham and hypocrisy; he loved justice and integrity. He was never too tired or too busy to sit down with a boy and his problems.

Each summer during my college years I raised a crop on my father's farm. In spite of this income, by the end of my sophomore year I was in debt several hundred dollars and decided to spend the next year teaching. I taught a five-month winter term and a six-week summer term in a one-room school in which I enrolled ninety students.

The younger children started to school in the early fall and the older ones came after crops were gathered. At first the trustees objected to my taking the older students. But when each of the older students agreed to teach some of the younger children in return for my teaching them, the trustees authorized their admission. About ten of them were older than I. Among them was one man thirty-seven years old who had three children in the school. Subjects which they studied included algebra, geometry, Latin, physics, and composition and rhetoric. In many ways this was one of the most rewarding years of work I have ever done.

My junior and senior years in college were somewhat better balanced than were the first two years. I stuck too close to books still but did find some time for outside activities, especially in athletics. Although I was planning to teach, I refused to accept the advice of the Dean of the College of Education, who urged me to take the professional education courses.

In April of my senior year I attended the annual meeting of the Alabama Education Association in Birmingham, at which time I received my appointment to a position to teach physics, chemistry, American history, medieval and modern history, plane geometry and solid geometry, and trigonometry in the high school at Selma, Alabama, and to coach football, basketball and baseball.

In Selma I found a very interesting community steeped in the culture and the philosophy of the Black Belt. My superintendent was an able schoolman who was generous in the time he gave to helping young teachers get started with their work. Two years as teacher and three as principal of the high school under his leadership were very valuable years in my life.

I served as superintendent of schools in Talladega and Selma, Alabama; Tampa, Florida; and Lynchburg, Virginia, before I came to Louisville in 1945. My stay (as teacher, principal, and superintendent) in Selma was eleven years. And I was in Lynchburg from 1932 to 1945.

My superintendent in Selma addressed his Negro teachers by their given names. There was considerable eyebrow raising in the community when as his successor I addressed them Miss, Mrs., or Mr., in the belief that they were entitled to this respect.

As principal of the Negro high school in Selma, we had an unusual man, R. B. Hudson. Not only was he a good principal but he was a very successful businessman as well. I relate the following incident involving him to underline the difficulties under which the educated, cultured Negro lived in Selma at that time.

The Hudson daughters attended college in Ohio and one of them in time was to be married to a successful young Negro doctor in Cleveland. Mr. Hudson came to me one afternoon to seek advice. He reminded me that when his daughter and her husband would leave Selma for Cleveland after their marriage they would have to ride the Negro car on the railroad and he wanted to know if I thought his white friends would misunderstand if he chartered a Pullman car to be attached to the train. He pointed out that it would enable the young couple to take with them their wedding gifts, which included some pieces of furniture and a grand piano which he and Mrs. Hudson were giving them. I sought the judgment of some older men in the community and we all agreed that this would not be misunderstood.

When I went to Tampa, Florida, in 1926, the Ku Klux Klan was in its heyday. The community was growing very rapidly and presented all the problems incident to rapid growth. While the Negro population was not large, perhaps 15 per cent, it seemed to me proper that we should have a Negro supervisor for the Negro work. There was vigorous objection to this on the part of some of the people of the community but a fine school board enabled this arrangement to continue.

My predecessor in Lynchburg, Virginia, was Mr. E. C. Glass, a brother of Senator Carter Glass. He served fifty-three years as superintendent, after serving eight years as principal. He was greatly beloved and admired by his brother the Senator. Senator Glass was one of the first to welcome me on my arrival in Lynchburg. This was the beginning of a warm friendship which lasted until his death. He owned, and his sons and his nephew operated, both the morning and the afternoon newspapers and many were the contacts I had with this family.

In the early days of public education in Lynchburg there were only white teachers for Negro schools. There was no stigma to teaching in the Negro schools. Mr. Glass' daughter taught Latin in the Negro high school for many years. When I went to Lynchburg in 1932 there had been no white teachers in the Negro schools for several years, but there were still no Negro principals. In general, Lynchburg schools were small, and each elementary principal served two buildings. That the Negro people might have no reason to feel they were assigned the less-good principals, I arranged for each principal in general to serve one white and one Negro school, and before leaving the system in 1945 had Negro principals of all Negro schools. The change was worked out gradually as retirements opened the way for it.

In the Lynchburg schools we had a rather complicated salary schedule based on teacher rating. It was severely discriminatory against the Negro teachers. Unable to get this discrimination removed, we gave Negro teachers as high ratings as conscience would permit, to compensate in some measure for the poorer schedule under which they were paid. When in time the courts ordered equalization of salaries without regard to race, we were confronted with a situation in which a goodly number of Negro teachers had "A" ratings when in reality they were less capable than many white teachers with "B" ratings.

163

As we developed a plan for equalizing Negro with white salaries over a three-year period, I had to face the responsibility of rerating the Negro teachers (lowering their ratings) because they were then rated in comparison with white teachers as well as one another. I invited all Negro teachers into conference and in the conference they matured, on their own initiative, a plan under which they created a committee with authority to bind the entire group in working out with the superintendent a formula for equalization of salaries.

They were assured that the equalization would be accomplished within a three-year period with no less than one third of the difference between the Negro and white schedules to be wiped out each year. We actually wiped out 40 per cent the first year, 40 per cent the second year, and 20 per cent the third year.

The N.A.A.C.P. came into the community exploring the possibility of bringing suit to require the superintendent to restore to Negro teachers their former ratings. The conviction of the Negro teachers that they had been treated fairly and justly was indicated by the fact that the N.A.A.C.P. attorneys found little encouragement among them and soon withdrew.

During my first year of teaching after graduation, I paid off the debts accumulated in my junior and senior years. The next year I began to fulfill the promise made my father when he helped me start my freshman year of college: that I would see that my sisters got an education. For a period of eleven years I had one, two, or three sisters in college each year. Their co-operation and good work in college and their success in later years made the keeping of this obligation both a satisfying experience and a high privilege.

When my sisters had completed their college work I could consider establishing a home of my own. In the fall of 1926, I married Elnora Blanchard of Montpelier, Vermont. Through four years in Tampa, thirteen in Lynchburg, and twelve in Louisville, she has been my constant challenge and inspiration, my severest critic and warmest supporter.

Two of the happiest years we knew, before our children came, were two we spent in New York. I was doing graduate work at Columbia and she research work at Cornell Medical College to finance us.

Happiest of all have been the years since the children came. All too quickly they grow up and are gone. Two are in college—one at Davidson and one at Vanderbilt. And one is married. Watching and helping them grow from infancy to maturity is a privilege which neither of us would have missed for anything else that life could have brought.

The coming of children into our home contributed, I like to think, to the effectiveness of my work as a school superintendent. There are some things we can better understand about other children through work with our own, and about other parents through our experiences as parents.

When I came to Louisville in July 1945, all the professional meetings—teachers, principals, supervisors and committees—were separate. There was, as noted earlier in these pages, no mixing of Negro and white teachers in meetings of any kind. Gradually, and always on as permissive a basis as possible, our professional meetings became mixed. Many of the early mixed groups were the result of completely voluntary action on the part of both Negro and white teachers.

I mention this again because it worked so well with the professional staff that permissiveness was developed as a major factor in the desegregation program for pupils, and I like to think that this was an important contribution to its success. Certainly, as our administrative staff well knows, it helped to produce the understanding, the patience, and the zeal with which our teachers, white and Negro, worked to make the program succeed—and without which even the best-made plans in the world might have foundered or failed.

Ours have not foundered or failed. I share the quiet pride of the community in their initial success. We have taken one good step toward enhancing the dignity of man. And that, in my humble opinion, is the treasure of which the Negro has most often been robbed, and which he thirsts most to possess. He must help himself, as he has helped himself, but he cannot do it all. For there is not true dignity but crippling gall when human worth walks the land unrecognized and even denied by others, and in a great nation where the dream and the promise (and more of the realization than anywhere else in the world) is summed up in two words—"citizens all"—it is the un-recognizing and the deniers who maim themselves as much as they maim their victims.

It is not difficult for me to believe that, since we are all children of the one God, surely there must be elements of greatness in every man. The elements may never be discovered, and so never fully or even partly realized. But their very existence is what at-tunes each of us to the presence of greatness in others, in life, and in the ideas that men live by.

In today's United States, which despite its imper-fections is the grandest result of man's capacity for greatness and for growth, there is one idea that nearly all men share. That is the supremacy of the law—its supremacy over the passions and prejudices of man that otherwise would reduce us to anarchy. There is another idea of equal power, less accepted by many, perhaps, and imperfectly written into our laws, but common to all our religions: justice for every individ-ual man, including his right to seek, unfettered, his place in the brotherhood of man.

In Louisville both of these powerful ideas in recent years and months have had fresh and uncommonly powerful exposition, and from many a quarter. They have not gone unheard.

I cherish the thought that a good many people in Louisville have expressed this year. For what has been done over the years and in this school year, and for the way in which it has been done, they say, the conscience of our community rests better. And in the schools there is a quiet pride: every child now has his chance.

APPENDIX

THE GENERAL FINDINGS of a public-opinion survey on
Louisville's school desegregation program are listed
on pages 147–149.

In making the survey the firm of Kemper & Associates employed twenty selected college students to
interview a representative cross-section of Louisville's
adult population (703 persons). Three Negro students interviewed the Negro respondents (sixteen per
cent of the total).

The following tables prepared by Kemper & Associates detail the wide diversity of opinion revealed
by the survey.

TABLE NO. 1

Estimated distribution of sentiment—within the Negro and white segments of the population, and for the population as a whole.

	WHITE segment	NEGRO segment	*Over-all population*
I am completely in favor of the new integration policy. The change should have been made in the Louisville schools a long time ago.	9.4%	50.2%	16.1%
I approve the new policy; it is both fair and sensible. Children, in publicly supported schools, should not be separated on the basis of skin color.	15.6	27.3	17.5
I believe that the change to a policy of integration in the schools was necessary. It was bound to come, sometime—and it will probably help save some of the cost of operating schools.	13.7	9.0	13.0
I really don't care much, one way or another.	8.7	1.4	7.5
I do not like the new integration policy. But the Supreme Court decision made desegregation the "law of the land"—and Louisville must obey the law.	14.6	2.6	12.6
I *do not approve* of the new desegregation policy. The Supreme Court went beyond its rightful responsibility with this decision. But, now that the change *has* been made in Louisville, I guess that nothing can be done, now, to change back to the old policy.	9.8	6.3	9.2
I am *completely opposed* to the desegregation policy. I think that the school people made a very serious mistake when they made this change. Louisville should change back to the old "separate but equal" schools for Negro and white children.	28.2	3.2	24.1
	100.0%	100.0%	100.0%

Male-female differences (basic opinion question); white segment of sample. (N = 589 respondents)

	MEN (N = 219)	WOMEN (N = 370)	Population Statistic: White (weighted)
I am completely in favor of the new integration policy. The change should have been made in the Louisville schools a long time ago.	10%	9%	9%
I approve the new policy; it is both fair and sensible. Children, in publicly supported schools, should not be separated on the basis of skin color.	12	19	16
I believe that the change to a policy of integration in the schools was necessary. It was bound to come, sometime—and it will probably help save some of the cost of operating schools.	14	13	14
I really don't care much, one way or another.	9	9	9
I do not like the new integration policy. But the Supreme Court decision made desegregation the "law of the land"—and Louisville must obey the law.	16	14	15
I *do not approve* of the new desegregation policy. The Supreme Court went beyond its rightful responsibility with this decision. But, now that the change *has* been made in Louisville, I guess that nothing can be done, now, to change back to the old policy.	11	8	10
I am *completely opposed* to the desegregation policy. I think that the school people made a very serious mistake when they made this change. Louisville should change back to the old "separate but equal" schools for Negro and white children.	28	28	28
	100%	100%	101% ("rounding error")

TABLE NO. 3

Breakdown in terms of *expressed religious preference;* respondents only. (N = 585 respondents) *

	CATHOLIC (N = 206) **	PROTESTANT (N = 369) **	JEWISH (N = 10) ***
I am completely in favor of the new integration policy. The change should have been made in the Louisville schools a long time ago.	12%	8%	31%
I approve the new policy; it is both fair and sensible. Children, in publicly supported schools, should not be separated on the basis of skin color.	16	15	31
I believe that the change to a policy of integration in the schools was necessary. It was bound to come, sometime—and it will probably help save some of the cost of operating schools.	9	15	7
I really don't care much, one way or another.	14	5	24
I do not like the new integration policy. But the Supreme Court decision made desegregation the "law of the land"—and Louisville must obey the law.	11	10	—
I *do not approve* of the new desegregation policy. The Supreme Court went beyond its rightful responsibility with this decision. But, now that the change *has* been made in Louisville, I guess that nothing can be done, now, to change back to the old policy.	11	17	—
I am *completely opposed* to the desegregation policy. I think that the school people made a very serious mistake when they made this change. Louisville should change back to the old "separate but equal" schools for Negro and white children.	27	30	7
	100%	100%	100%

* Three respondents (all women) indicated that they had no religious preference; they are not included in this breakdown.
** In all three groups, we weighted the statistics to equate the male-female proportions.
*** The number of Jewish respondents is so small that we do not consider the percentage statistics to have any sort of significance as valid predictors.

TABLE NO. 4

Parks and Swimming Pools
"How do you feel about the use of the city swimming pools and the city parks?"

| | "Do you think that all city parks should be open to Negroes?" | | | "Do you think that all city swimming pools should be open to Negroes?" | | |
| | PARKS | | | POOLS | | |
	yes	?	no	yes	?	no
Over-all Population Statistic (weighted)	38%	8%	54%	29%	6%	65%
Negro segment of the sample (weighted)	88%	4%	8%	88%	3%	9%
White segment of the sample (weighted)	28%	9%	63%	17%	6%	77%
Negro respondents:						
Men (N = 40)	85%	5%	10%	85%	5%	10%
Women (N = 75)	91%	3%	7%	91%	1%	8%
White respondents:						
Men (N = 218)	31%	6%	63%	21%	4%	75%
Women (N = 370)	25%	12%	63%	14%	9%	77%

NOTE: Where indicated, the statistics have been "weighted" to equate the impact made on the total statistic by each sex.

ABOUT THE AUTHORS

OMER CARMICHAEL *was born sixty-four years ago on a farm in the pine-and-cotton country of Clay County, in Alabama. By the time he was nine he was plowing in the spring, and when he went away to college at the University of Alabama his father gave him $125 in cash and free use of land to make a crop each summer. He became a teacher and then a school superintendent, serving in various towns and cities of the South before going to Louisville in 1945. He is married and has three children.*

WELDON JAMES *is associate editor of the Louisville* Courier-Journal, *which gave him a leave of absence to write this book. He has been a foreign correspondent, a Nieman Fellow at Harvard, an editor of* Collier's, *a lieutenant colonel in the Marine Corps. He is also married, with three children. This is the first book for each of its authors.*